JAZZ MASTERS PLAY
GERSHWIN

GERSHWIN® and GEORGE GERSHWIN® are registered trademarks of Gershwin Enterprises
IRA GERSHWIN™ is a trademark of Gershwin Enterprises
PORGY AND BESS® is a registered trademark of Porgy And Bess Enterprises

Music transcriptions by Jeff Jacobson and Pete Billmann

ISBN 978-1-4803-1285-2

HAL•LEONARD®
CORPORATION
7777 W. BLUEMOUND RD. P.O. BOX 13819 MILWAUKEE, WI 53213

In Australia Contact:
Hal Leonard Australia Pty. Ltd.
4 Lentara Court
Cheltenham, Victoria, 3192 Australia
Email: ausadmin@halleonard.com.au

Visit Hal Leonard Online at
www.halleonard.com

But Not for Me
Music and Lyrics by George Gershwin and Ira Gershwin

Drop D tuning:
(low to high) D-A-D-G-B-E

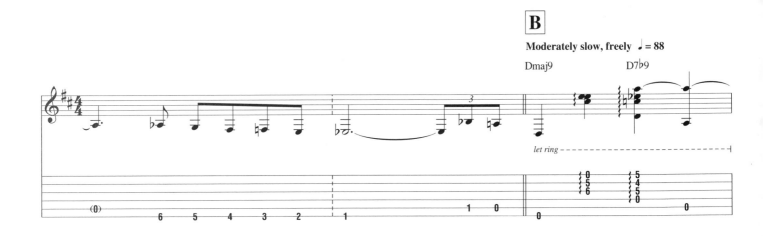

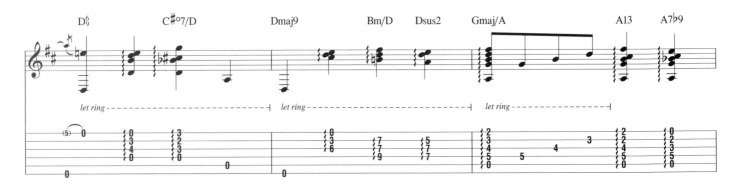

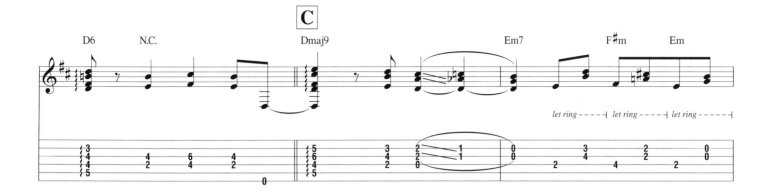

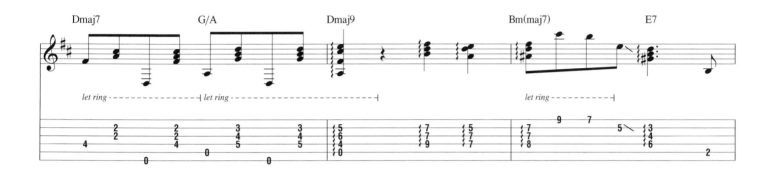

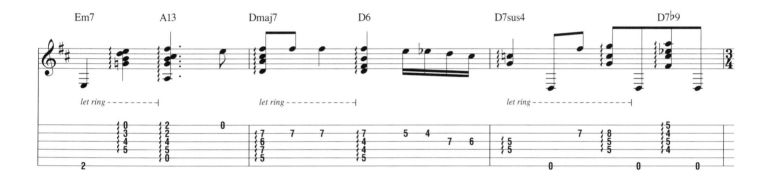

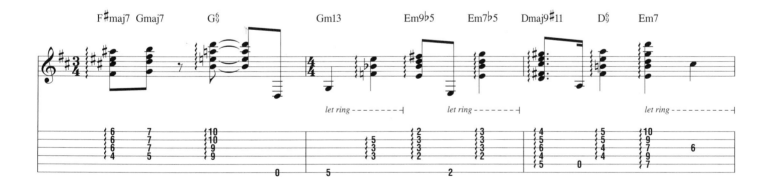

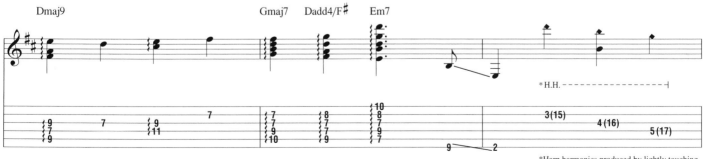

*Harp harmonics produced by lightly touching string 12 frets above fretted note while picking string.

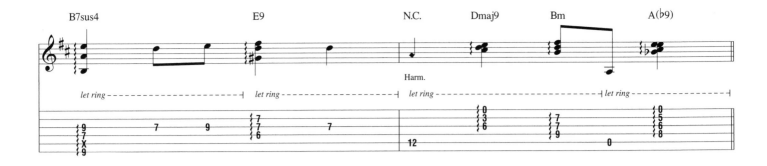

D

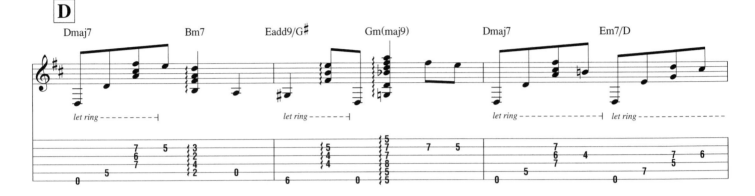

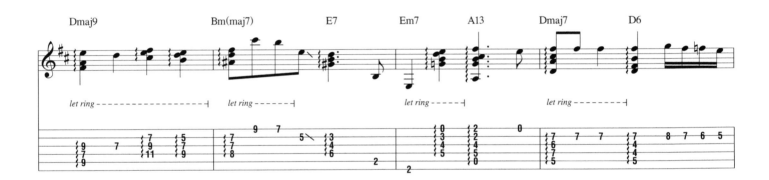

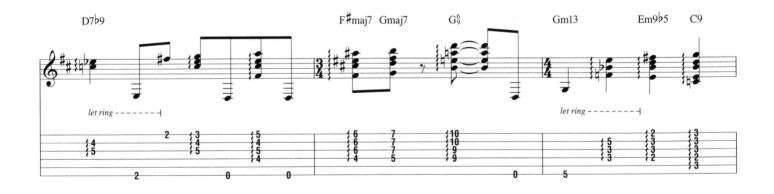

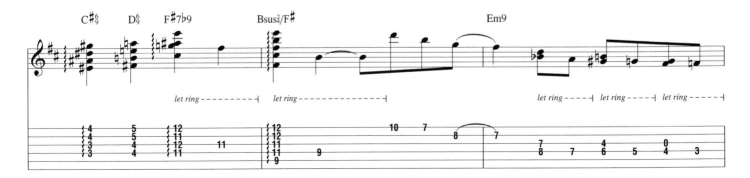

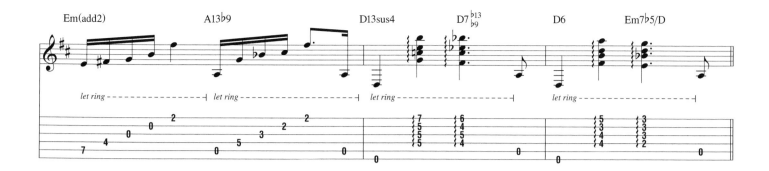

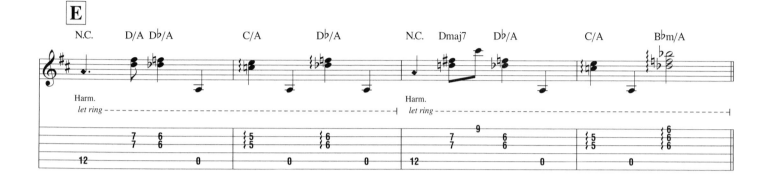

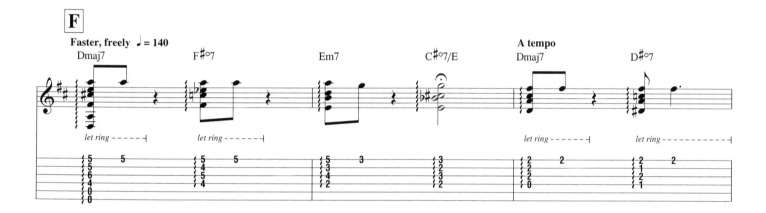

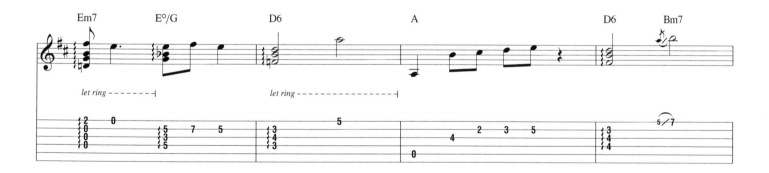

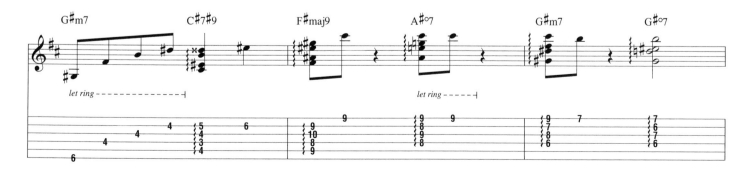

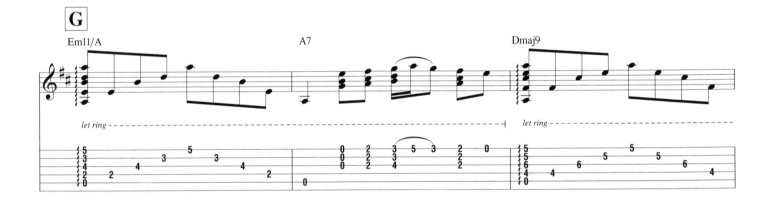

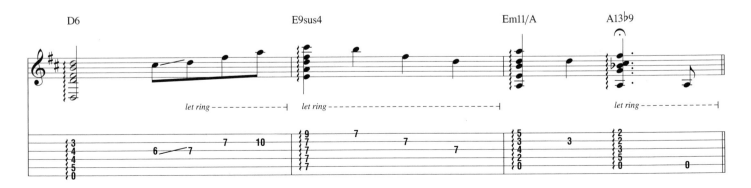

*Harp harmonics produced by touching
strings w/ palm edge of pick hand
approx. 12 frets above fretted notes
while picking strings.

Embraceable You

Music and Lyrics by George Gershwin and Ira Gershwin

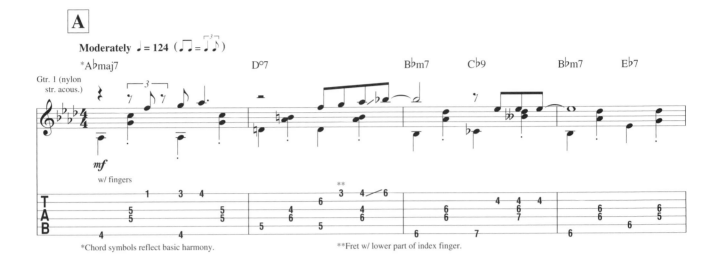

*Chord symbols reflect basic harmony.   **Fret w/ lower part of index finger.

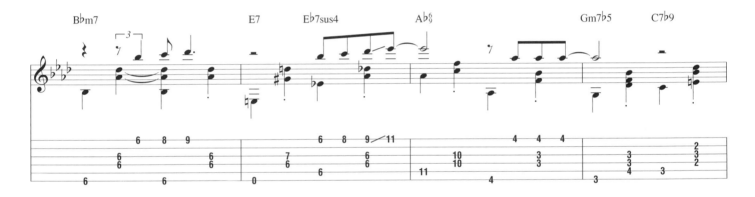

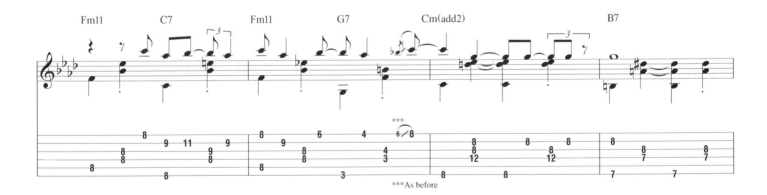

***As before

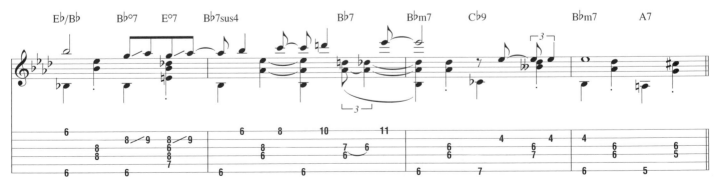

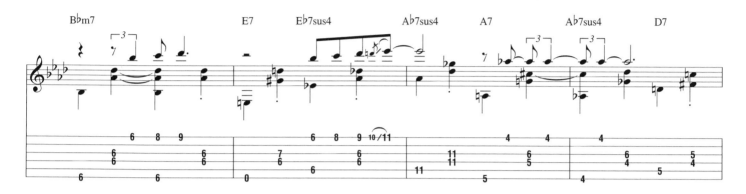

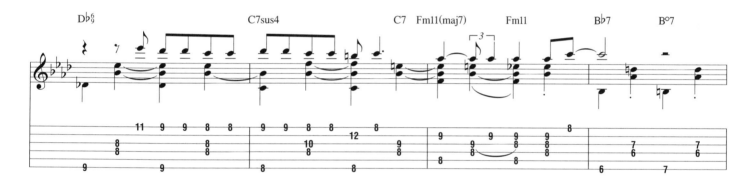

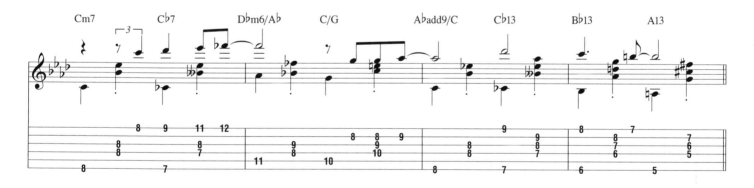

*Played as even eighth notes.

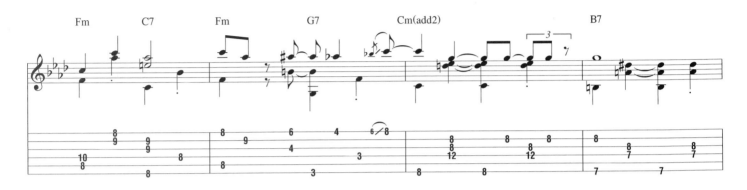

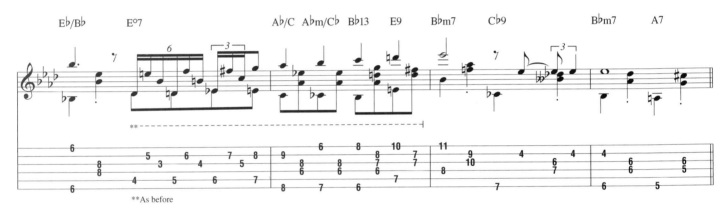

**As before

***As before

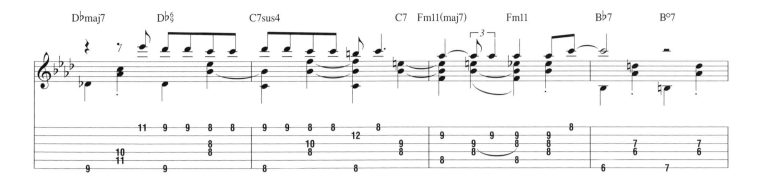

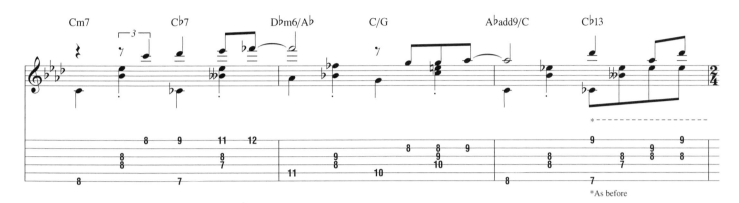

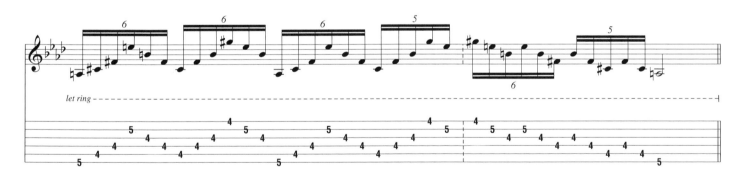

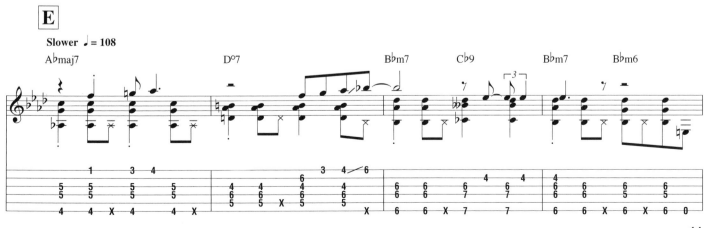

11

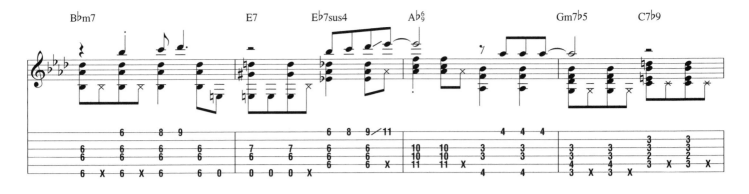

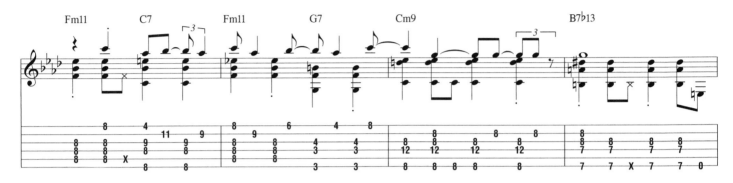

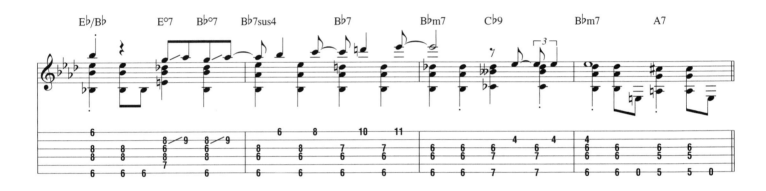

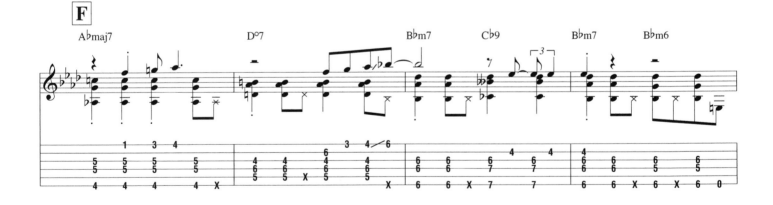

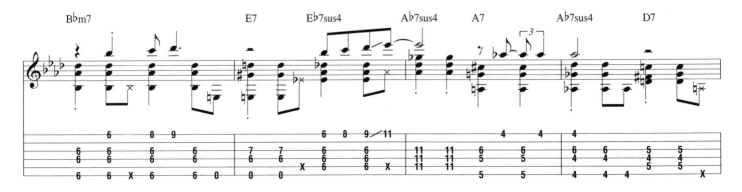

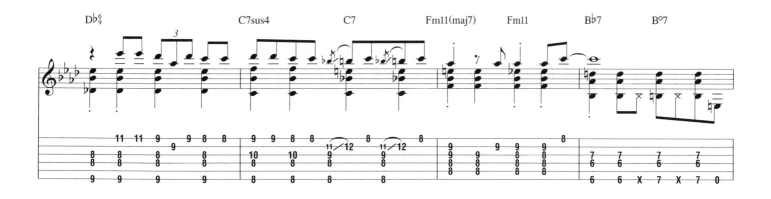

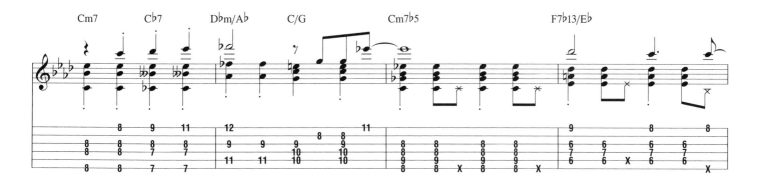

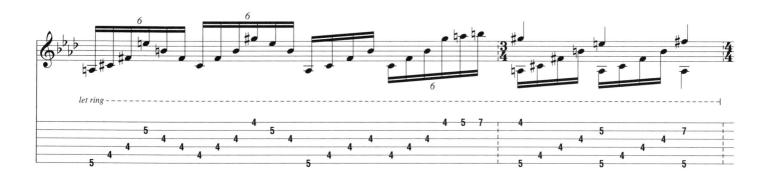

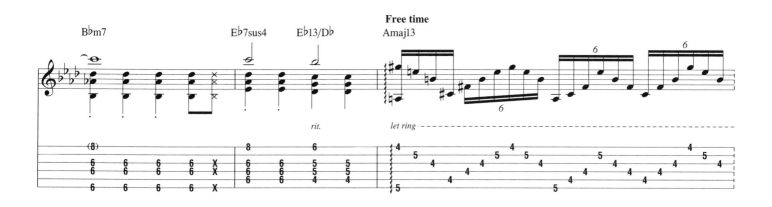

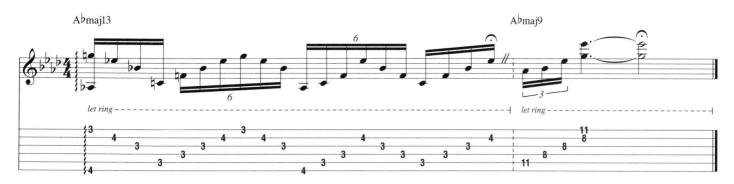

A Foggy Day (In London Town)

Music and Lyrics by George Gershwin and Ira Gershwin

7-str. gtr.: Drop A tuning, down 1 step:
(low to high) G-D-G-C-F-A-D

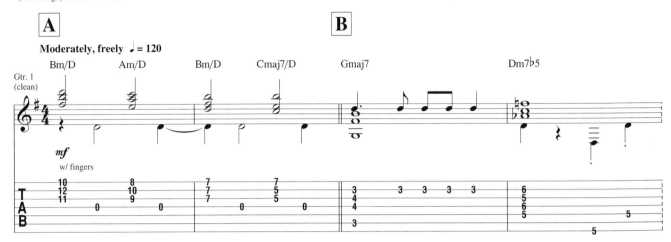

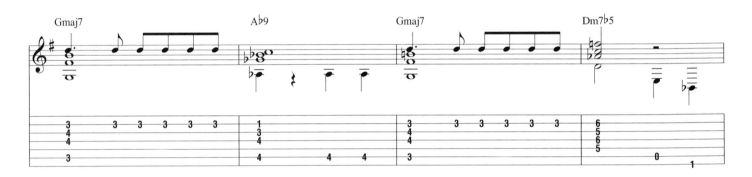

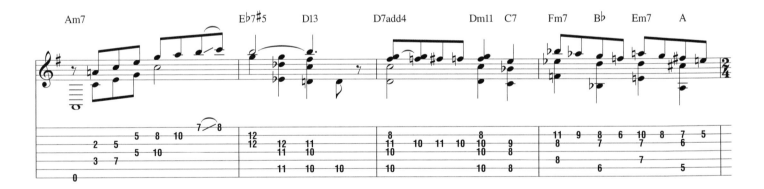

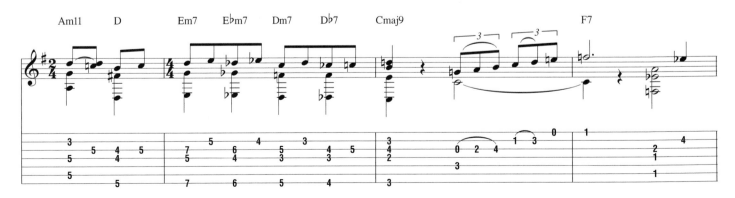

*For 5-note chords, pluck top note w/ pinky.

C

Faster ♩ = 140

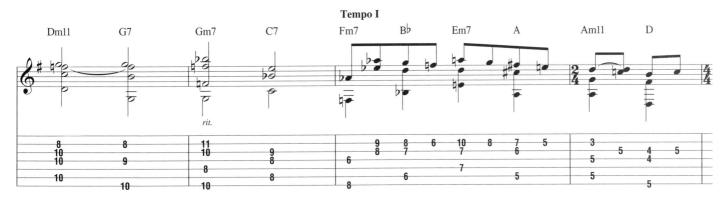

**Fret top note w/ lower part of index finger.

Tempo I

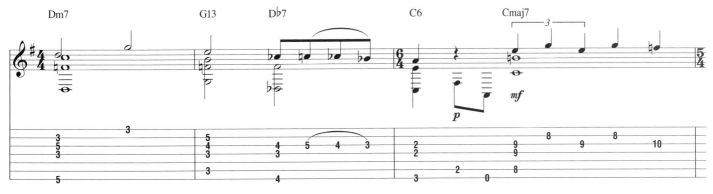

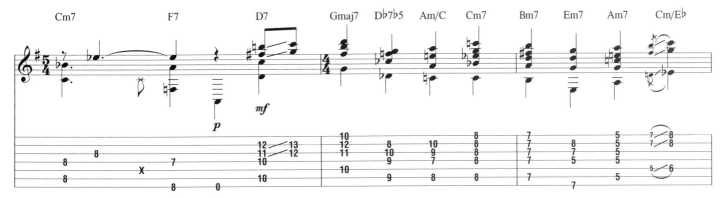

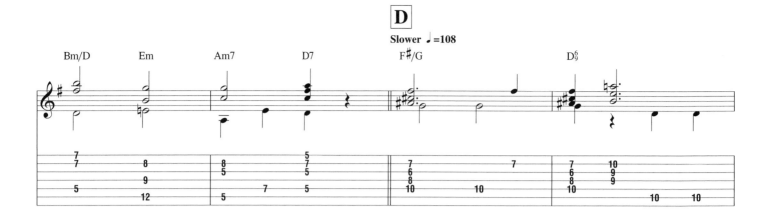

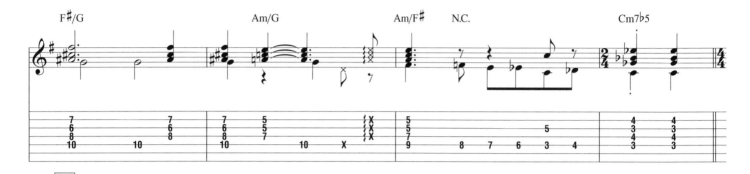

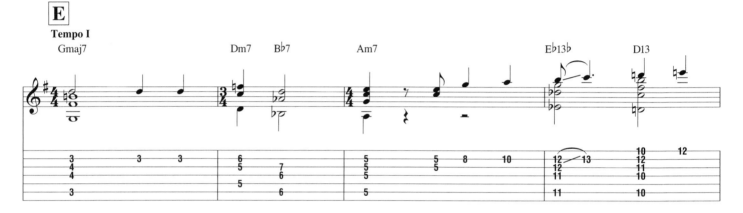

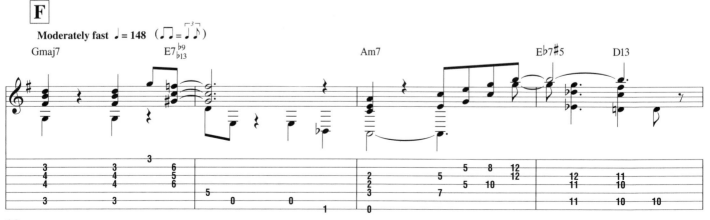

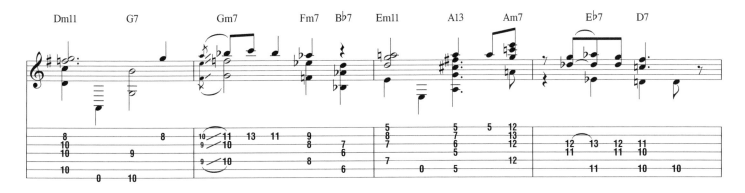

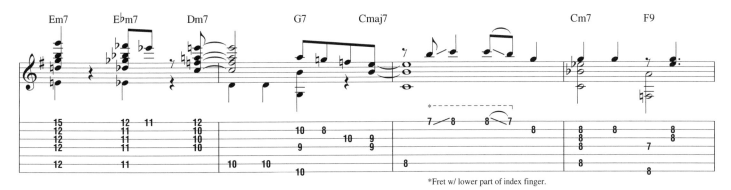

*Fret w/ lower part of index finger.

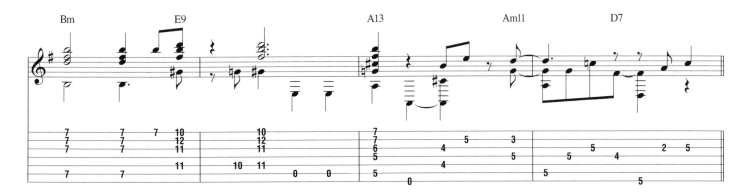

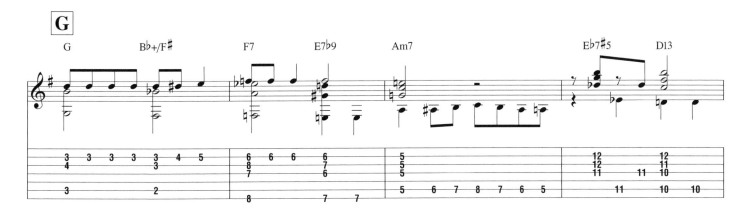

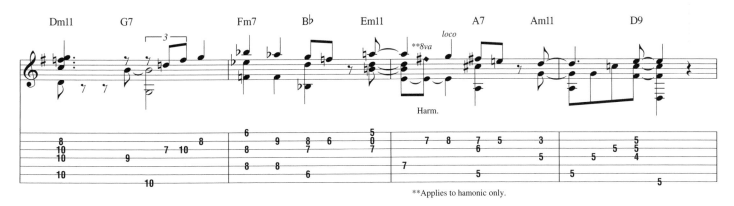

**Applies to hamonic only.

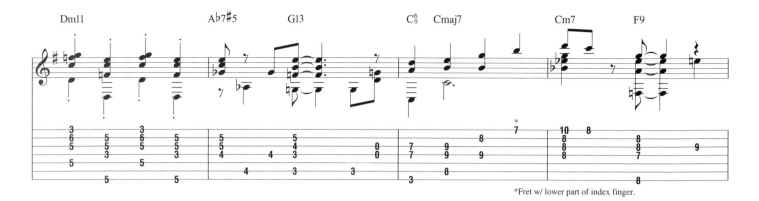

*Fret w/ lower part of index finger.

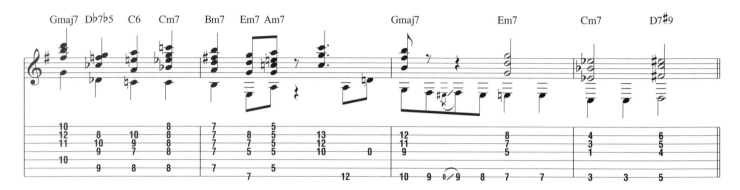

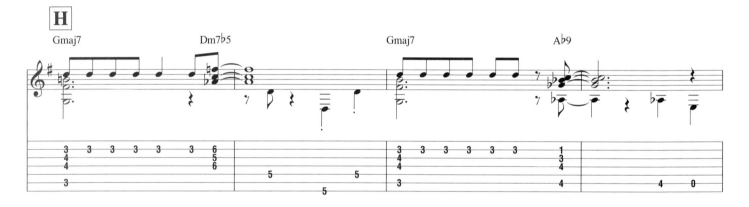

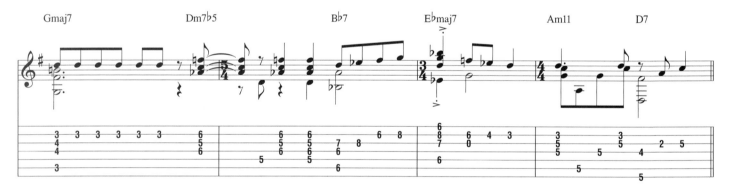

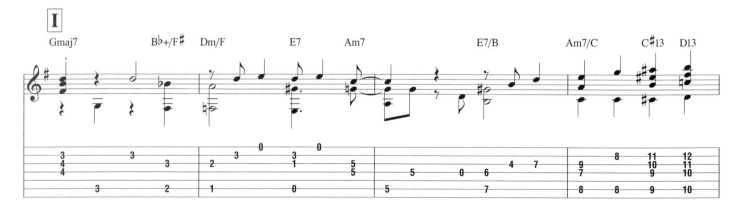

*Fret w/ lower part of index finger.

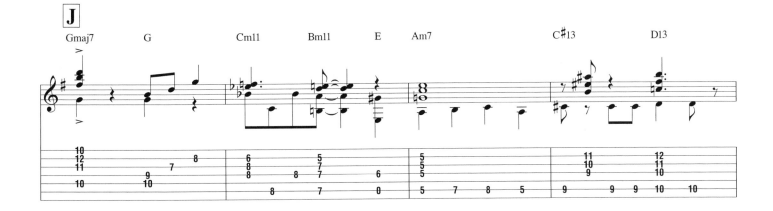

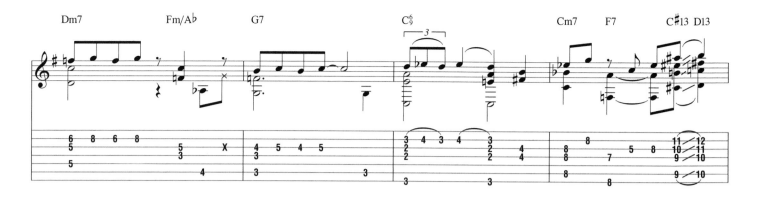

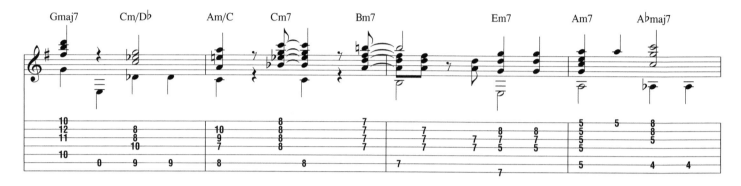

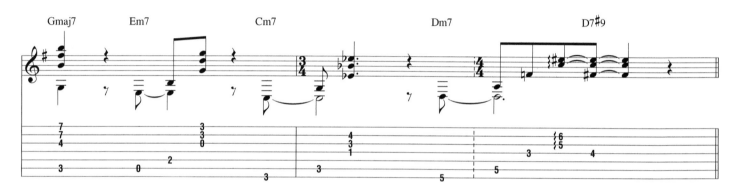

K

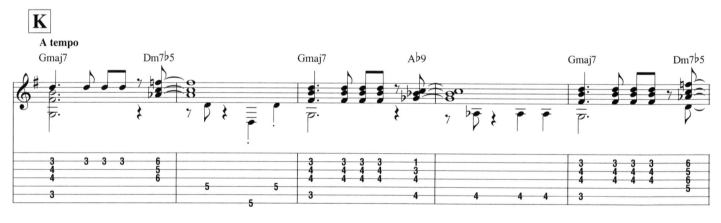

L

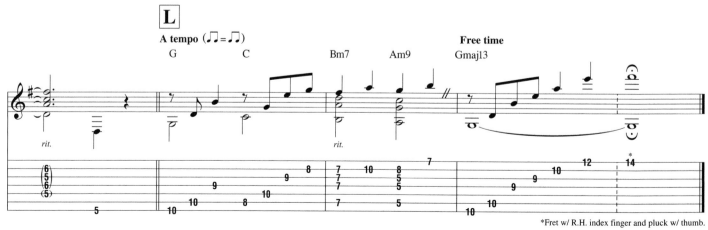

*Fret w/ R.H. index finger and pluck w/ thumb.

from Martin Taylor - *The Best of Martin Taylor*

I Got Rhythm

Music and Lyrics by George Gershwin and Ira Gershwin

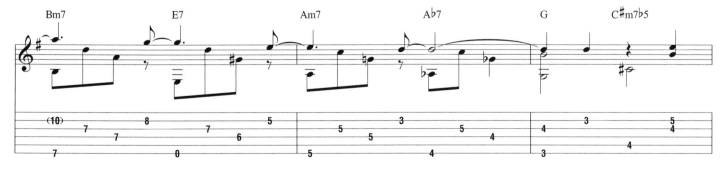

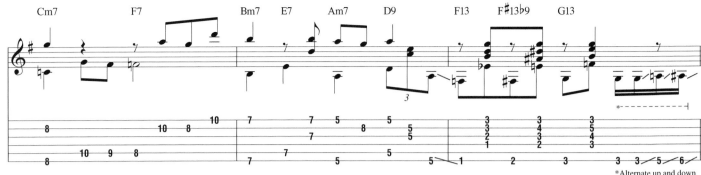

*Alternate up and down strokes w/ thumb.

B

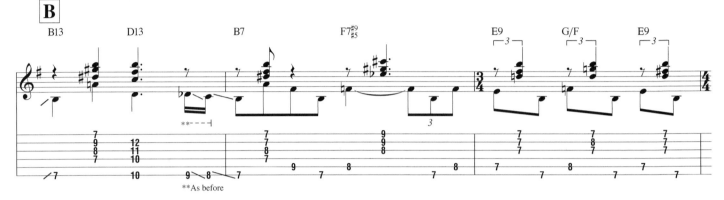

**As before

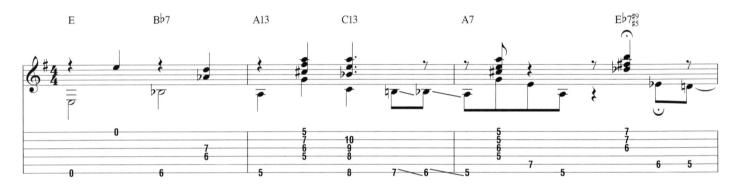

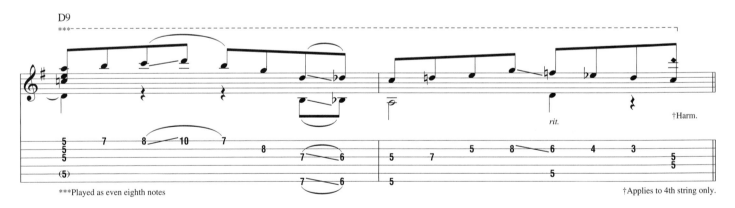

***Played as even eighth notes

†Applies to 4th string only.

rit.

†Harm.

C

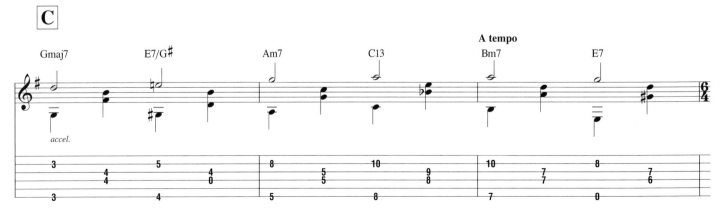

A tempo

accel.

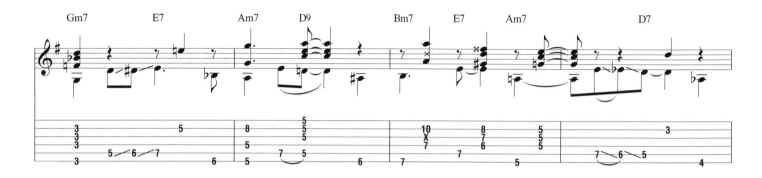

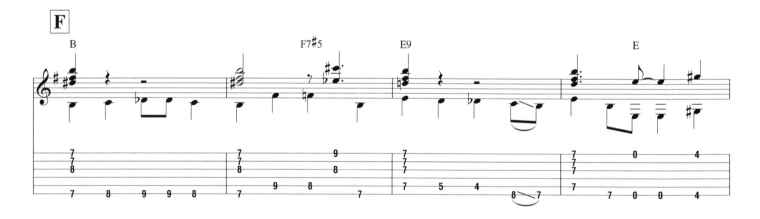

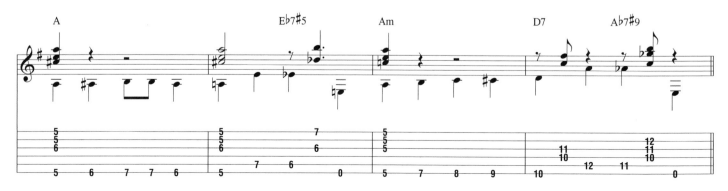

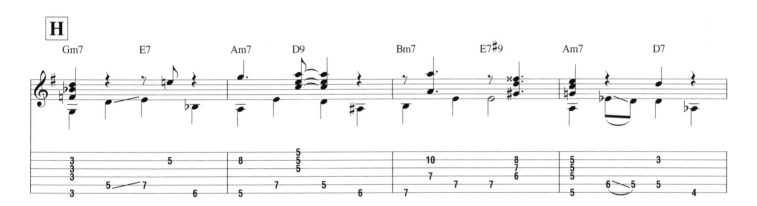

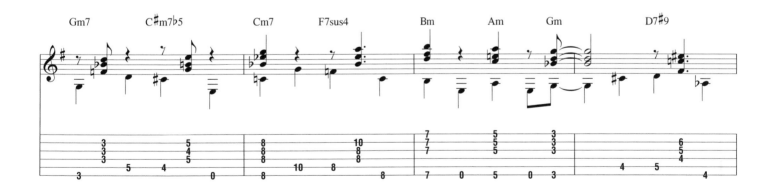

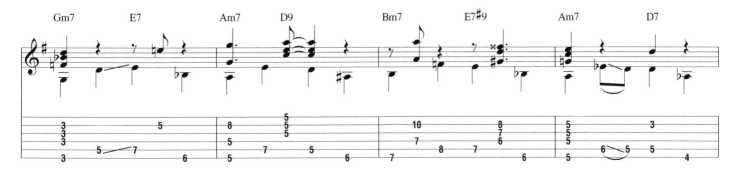

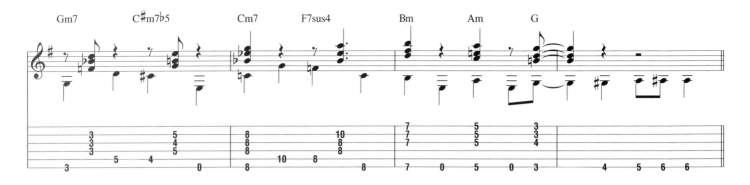

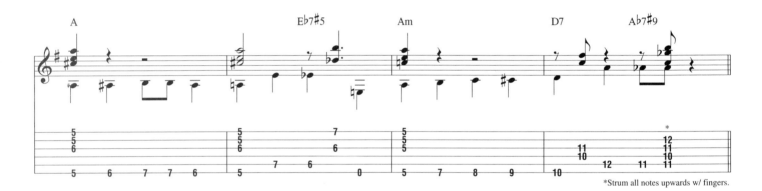

*Strum all notes upwards w/ fingers.

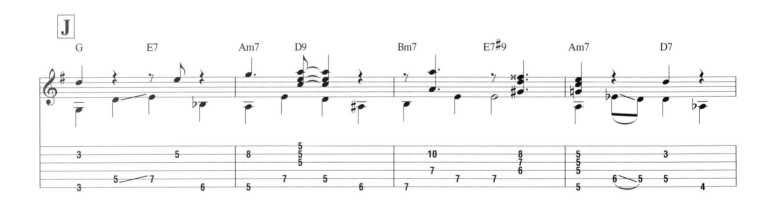

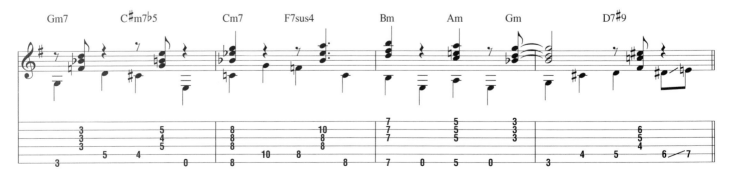

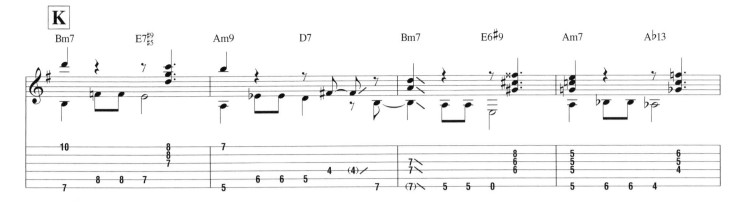

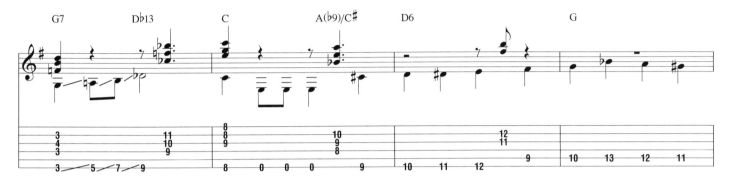

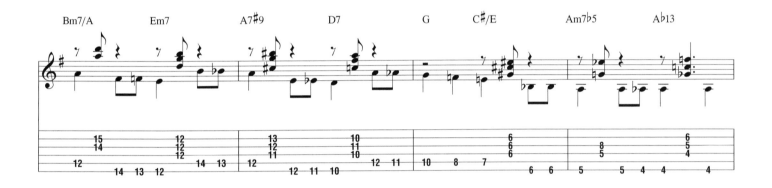

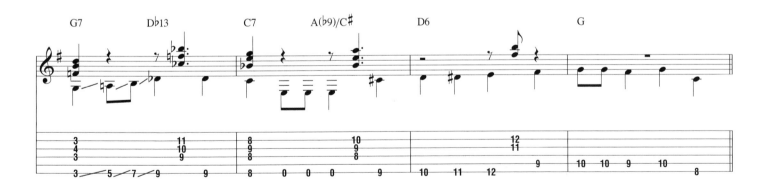

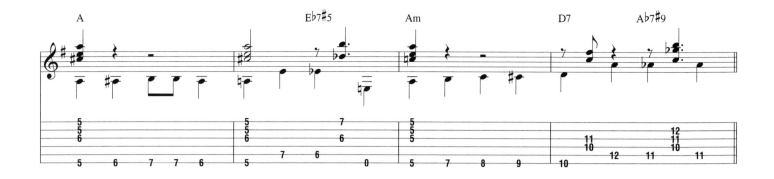

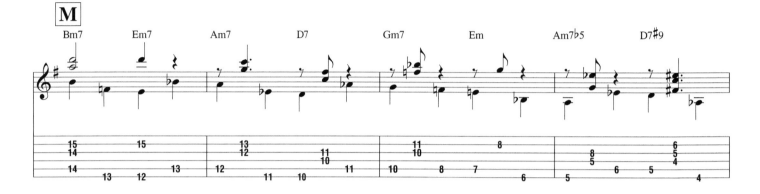

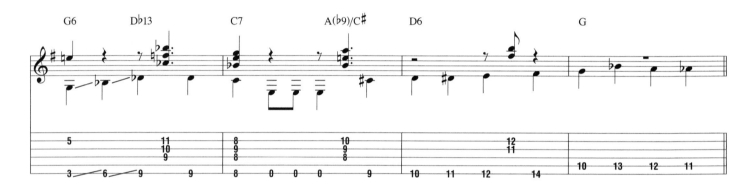

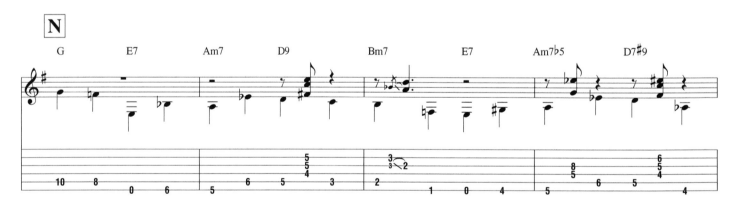

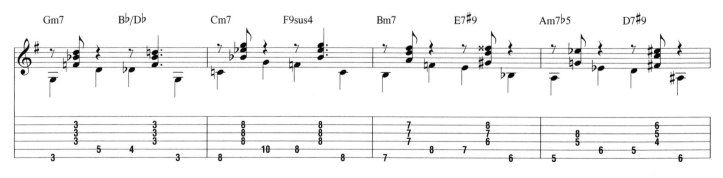

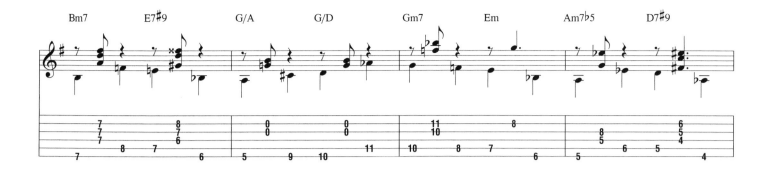

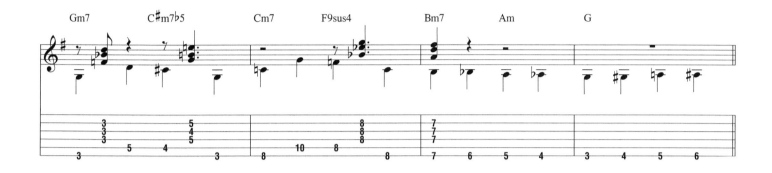

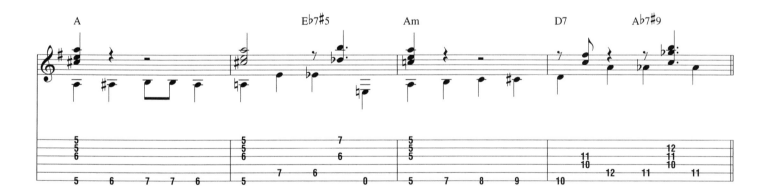

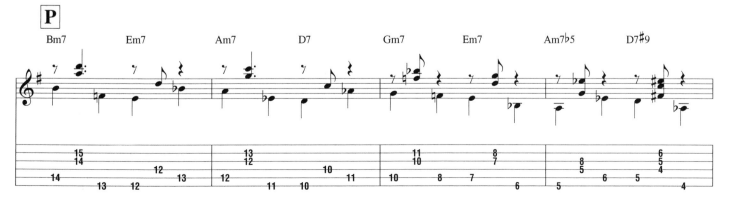

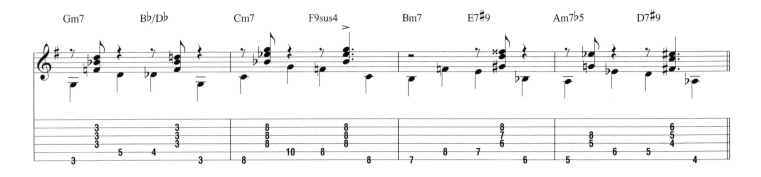

Q

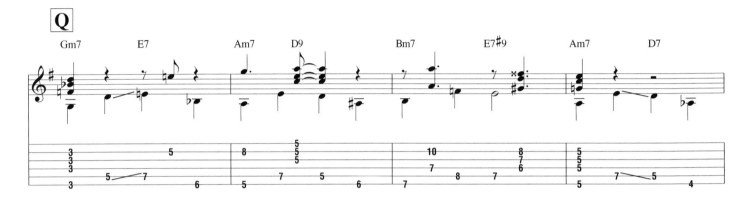

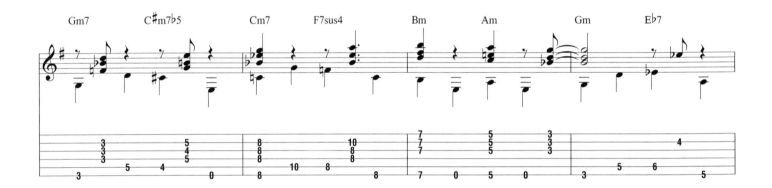

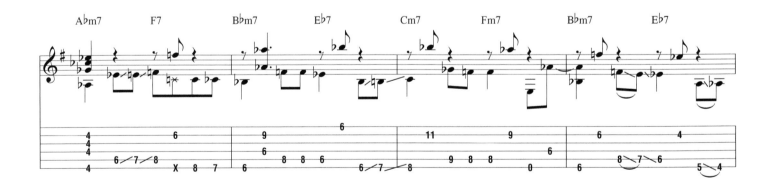

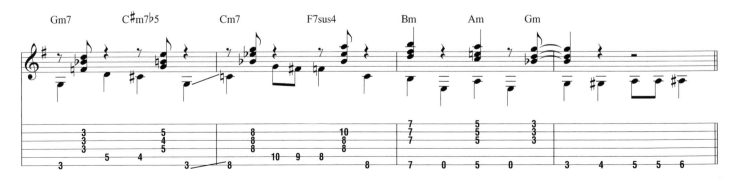

from Johnny Smith - *The Man with the Blue Guitar*

I Loves You, Porgy

from PORGY AND BESS

Music and Lyrics by George Gershwin, DuBose and Dorothy Heyward and Ira Gershwin

Drop D tuning:
(low to high) D-A-D-G-B-E

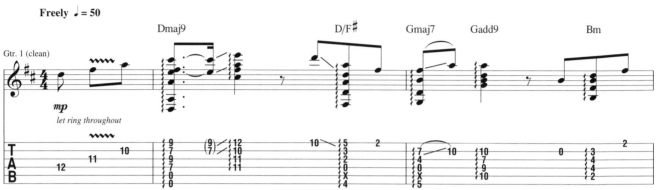

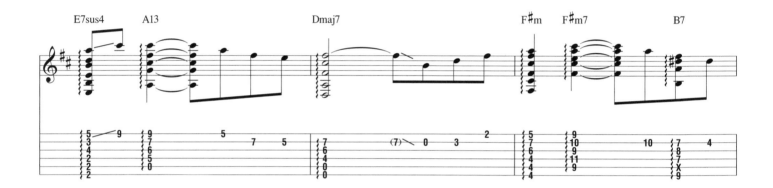

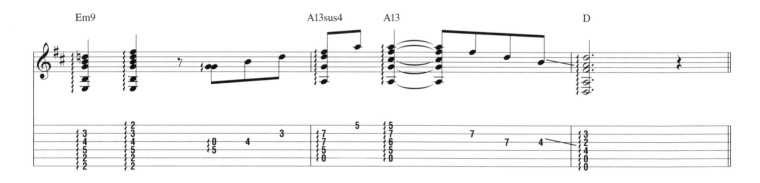

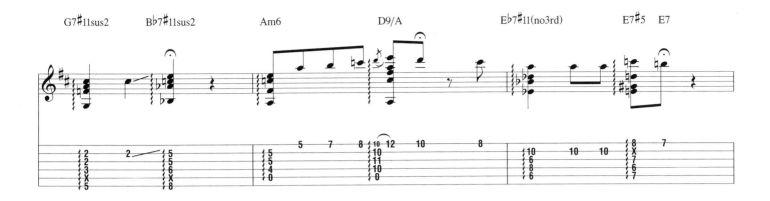

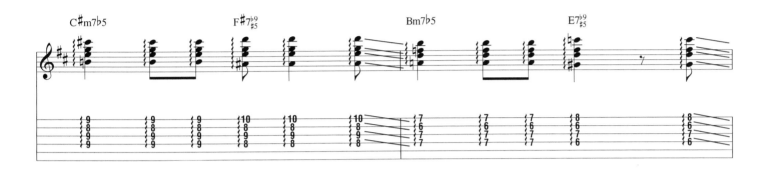

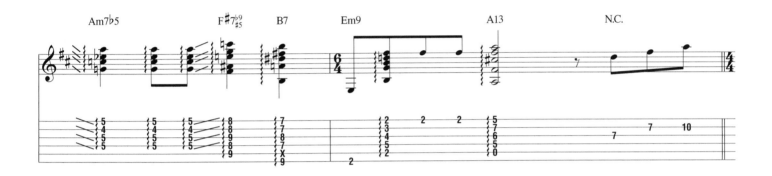

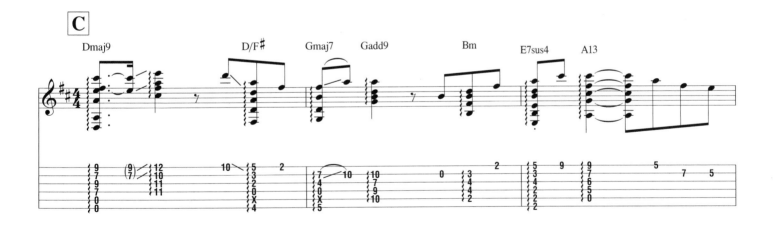

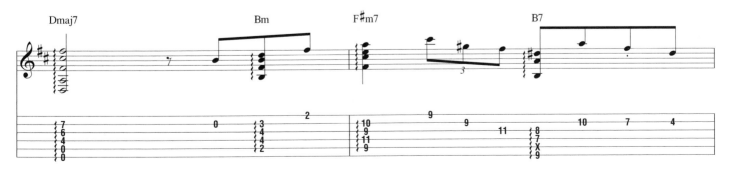

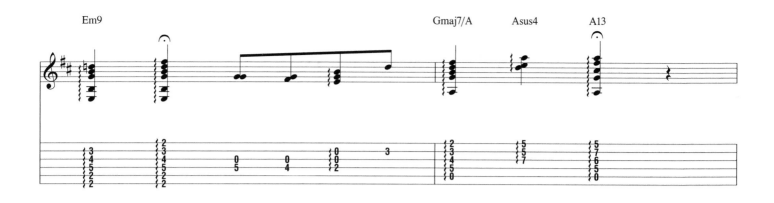

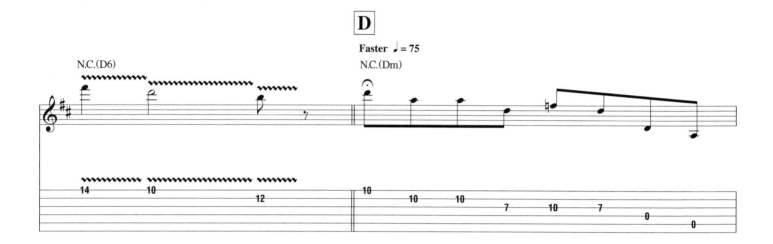

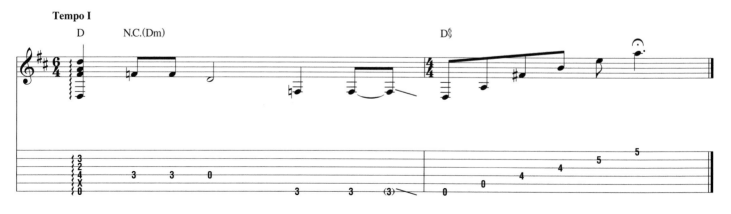

Isn't It a Pity?

Music and Lyrics by George Gershwin and Ira Gershwin

Tuning:
(low to high) A-E-A-D-G-B-E

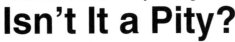

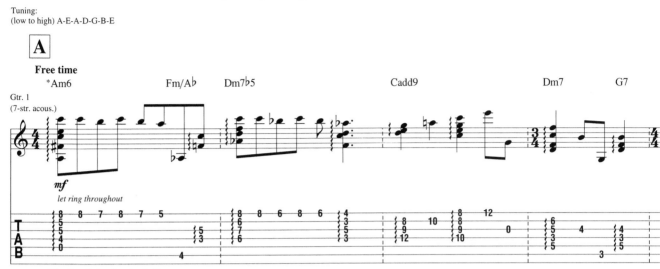

*Chord symbols reflect implied harmony.

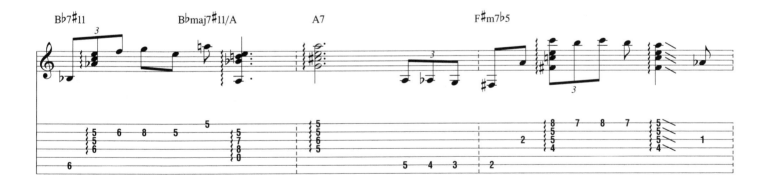

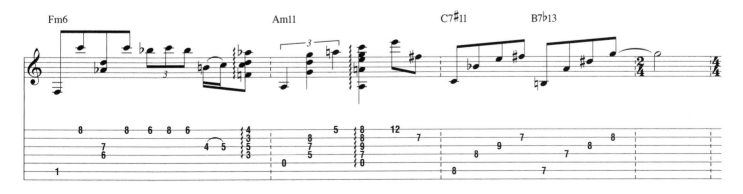

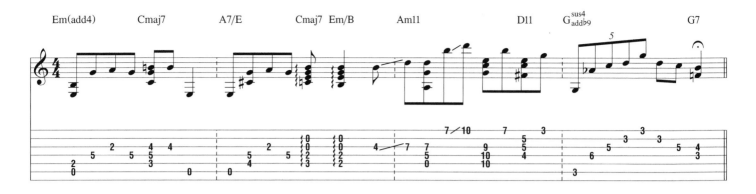

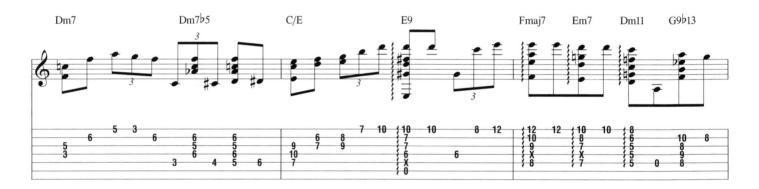

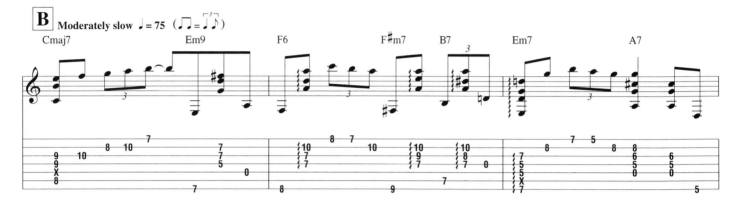

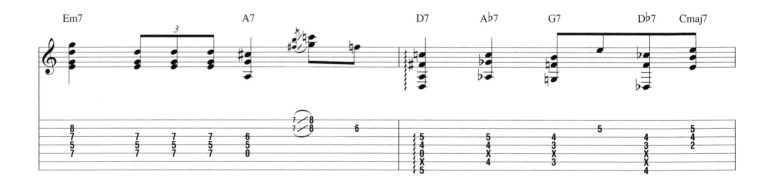

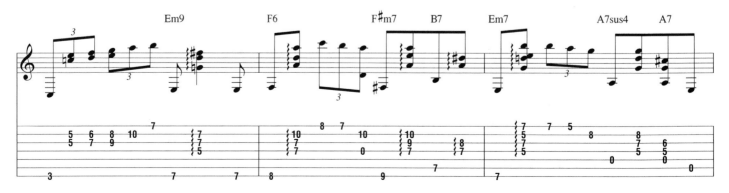

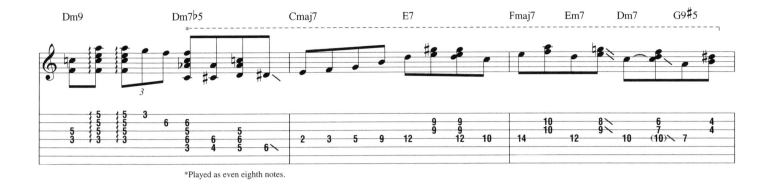

*Played as even eighth notes.

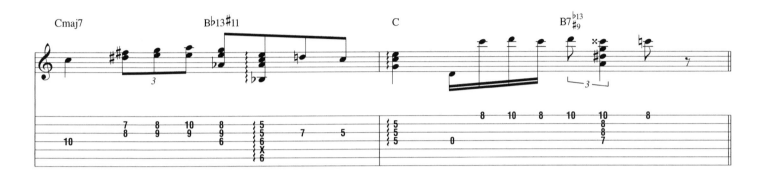

C

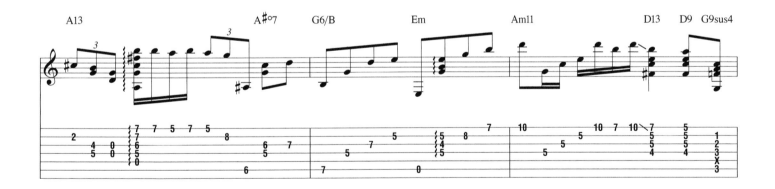

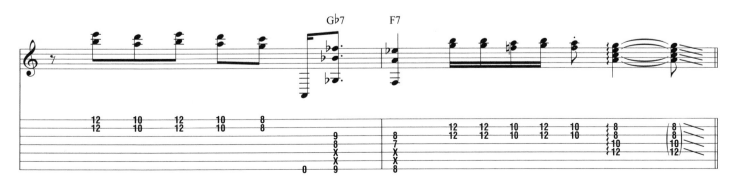

D

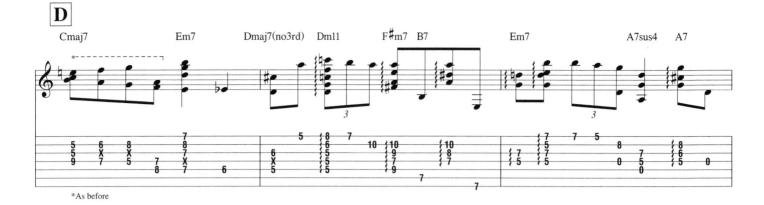

*As before

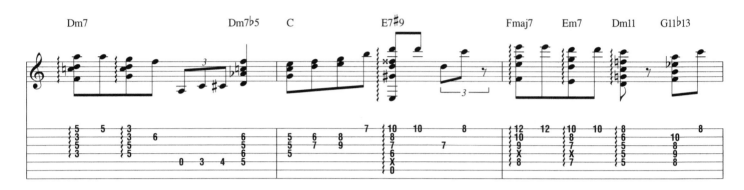

E

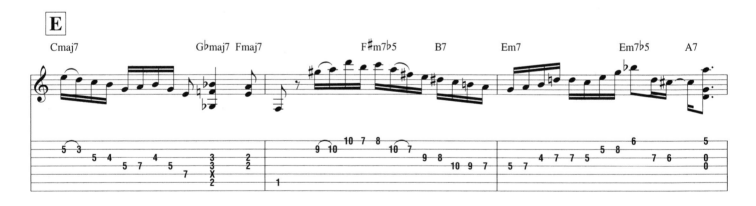

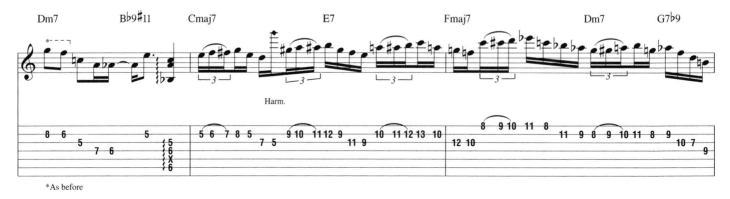

*As before

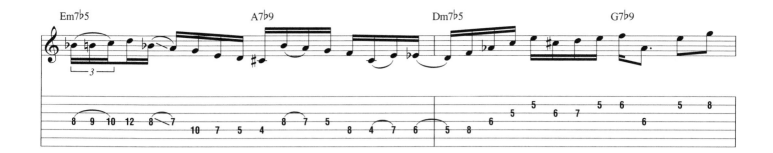

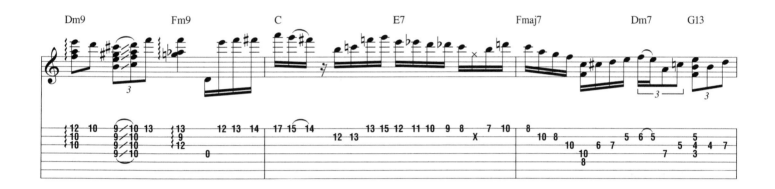

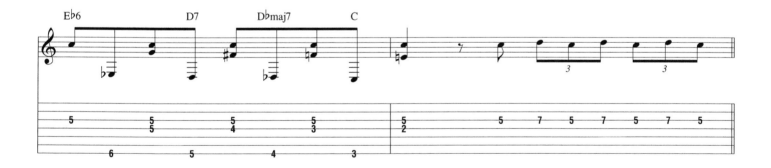

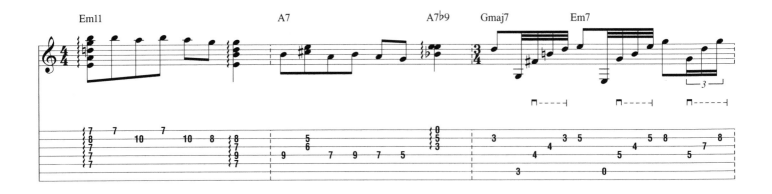

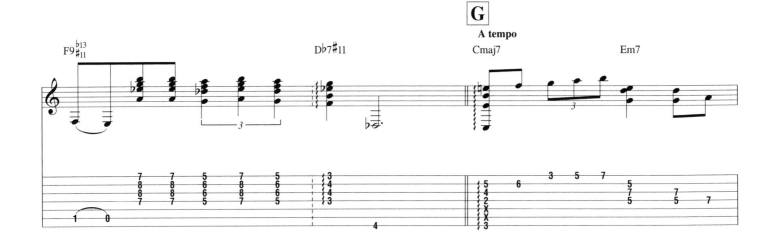

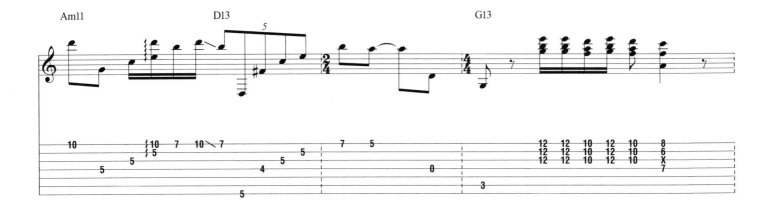

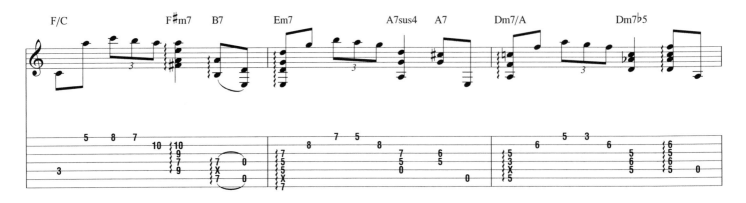

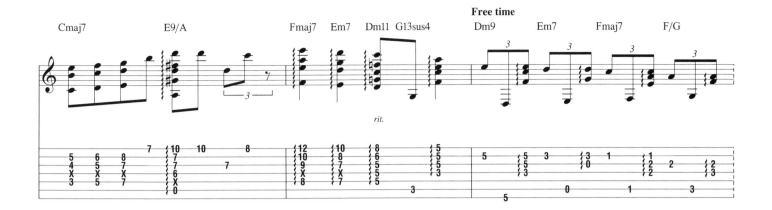

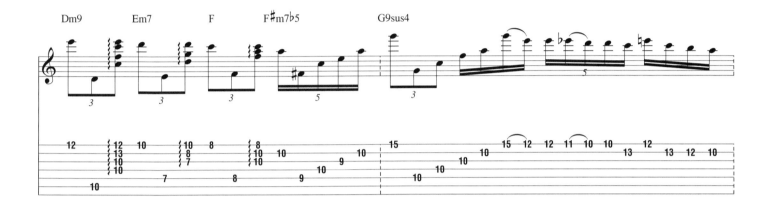

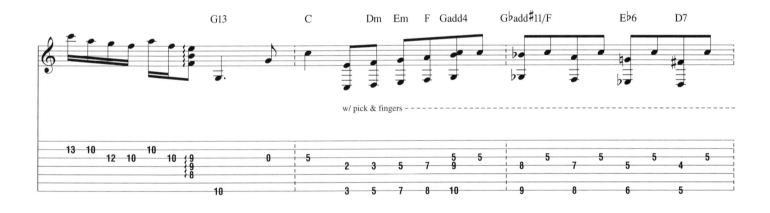

from Ralph Towner - *Time Line*

My Man's Gone Now

from PORGY AND BESS

Words and Music by George Gershwin, DuBose and Dorothy Heyward and Ira Gershwin

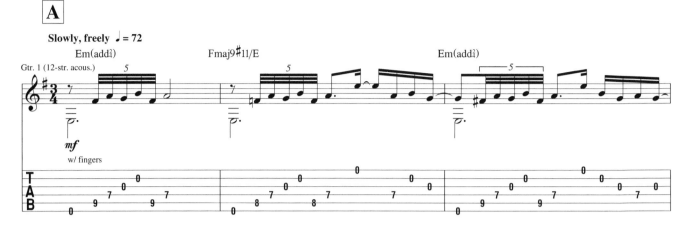

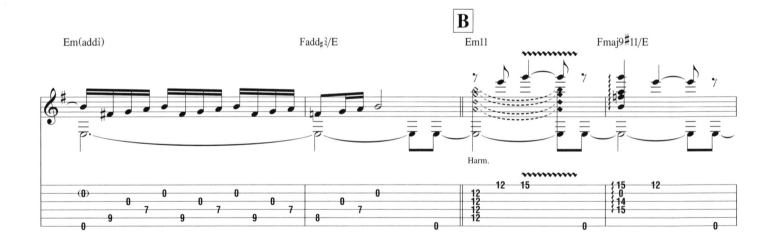

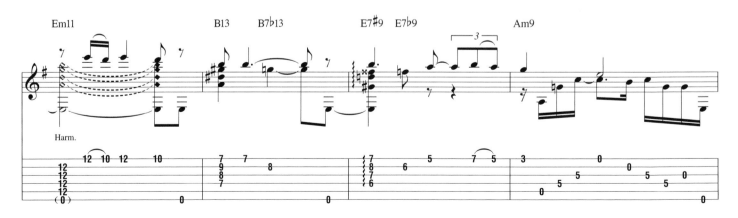

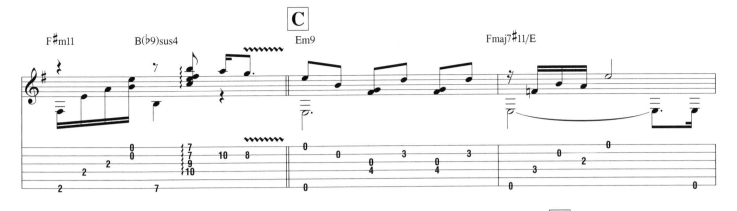

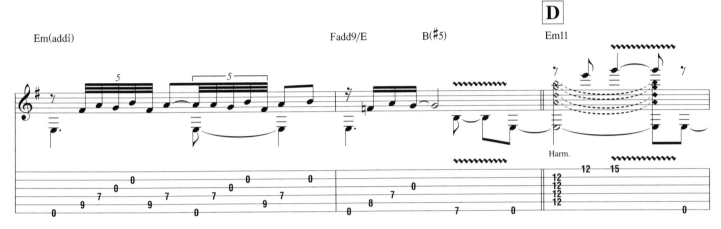

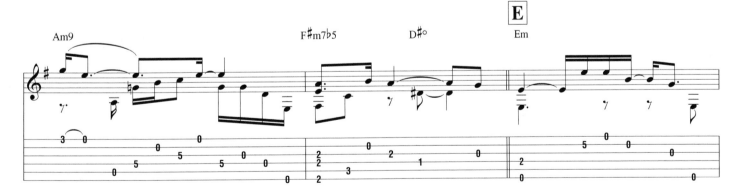

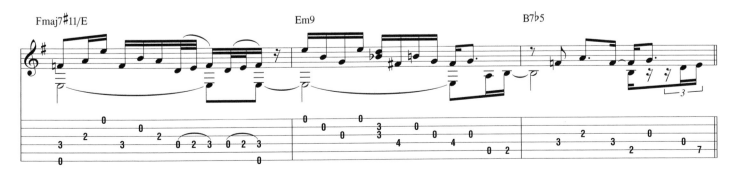

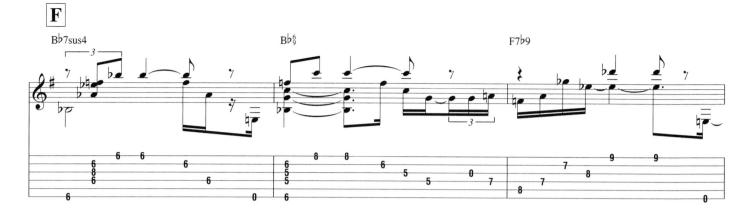

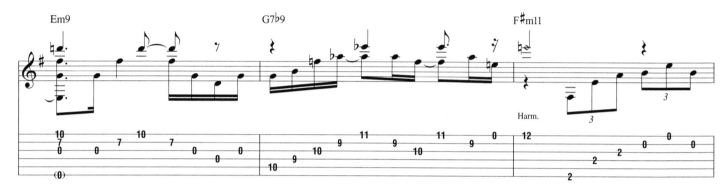

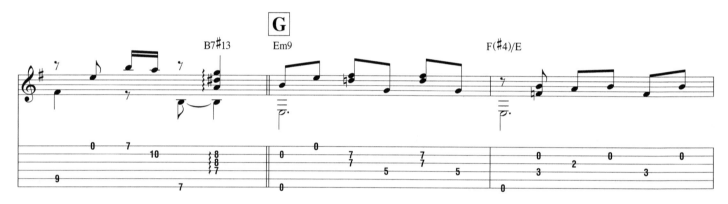

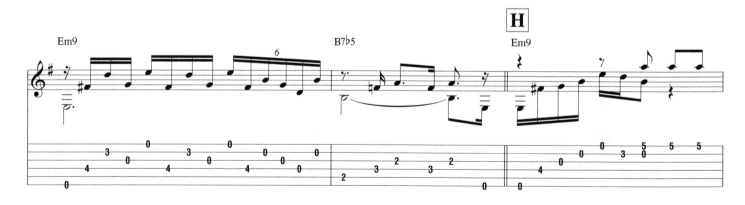

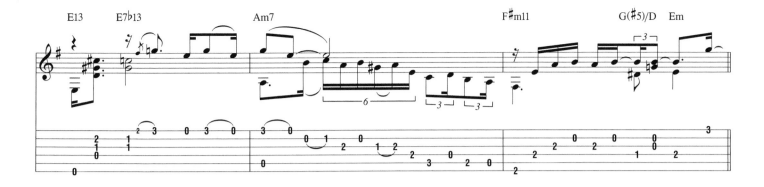

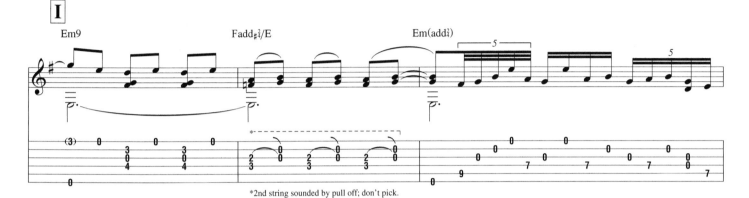

*2nd string sounded by pull off; don't pick.

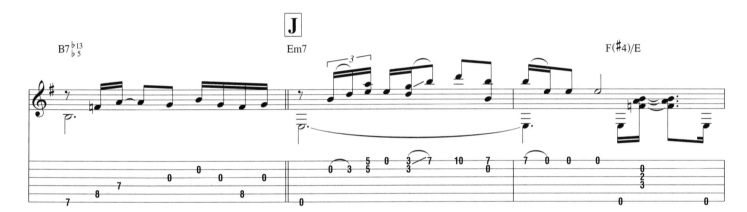

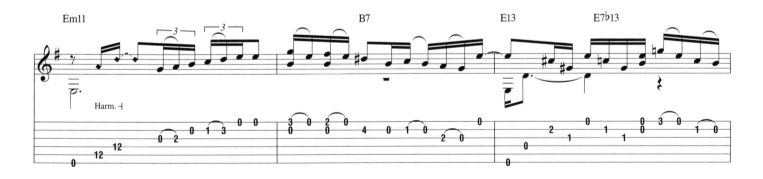

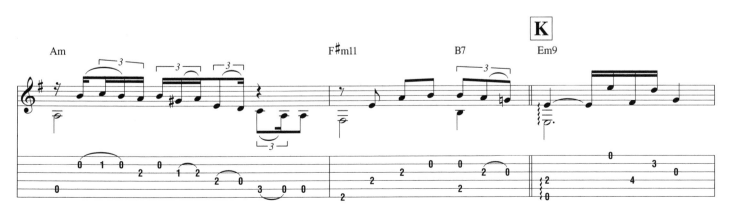

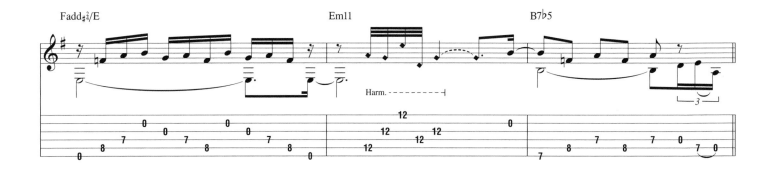

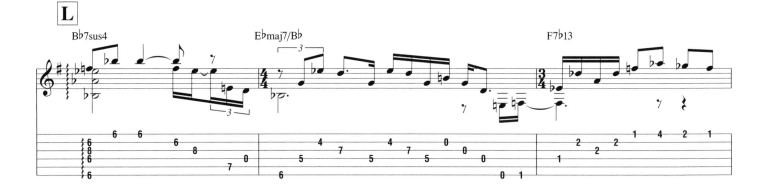

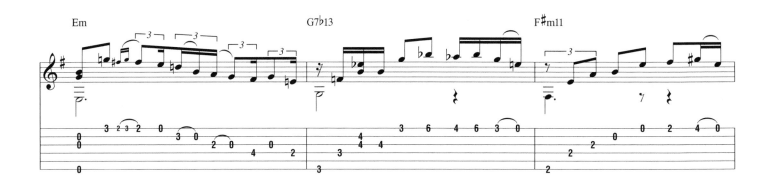

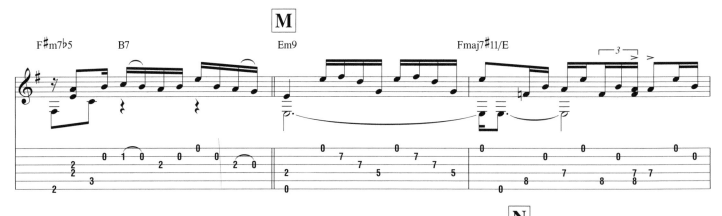

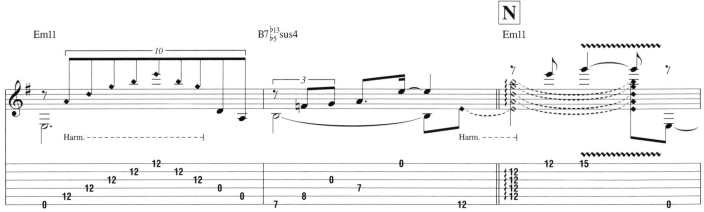

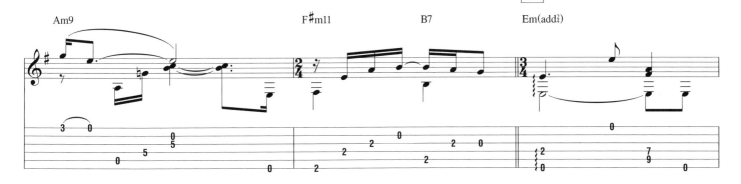

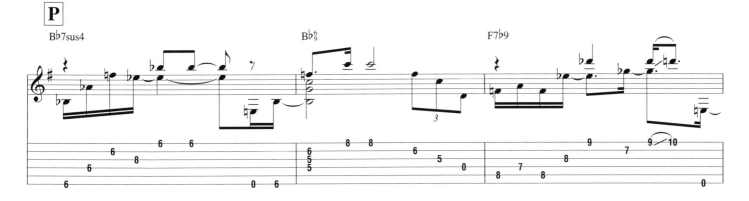

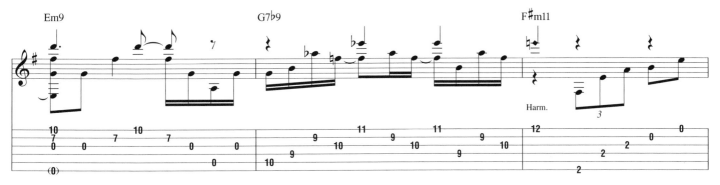

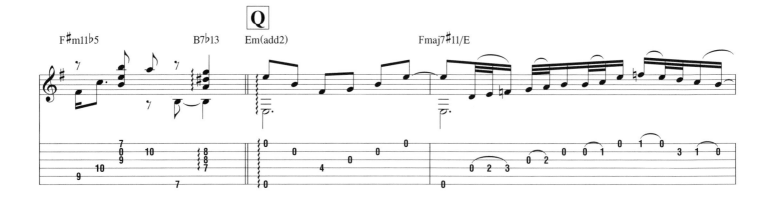

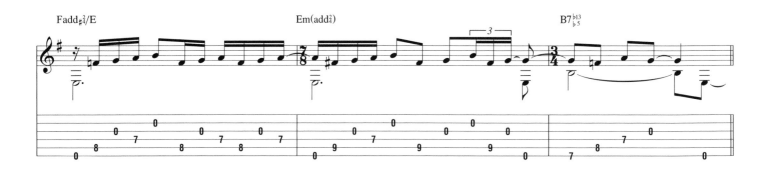

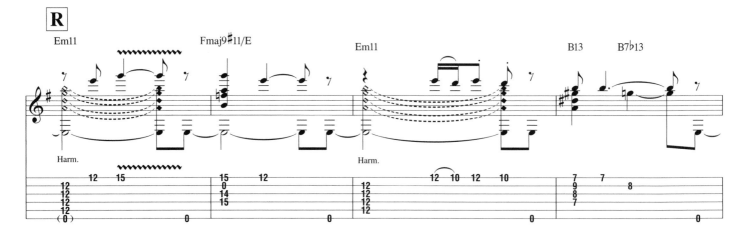

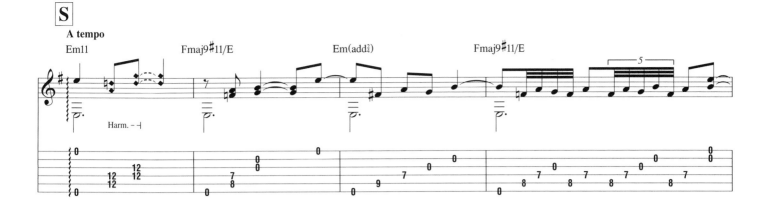

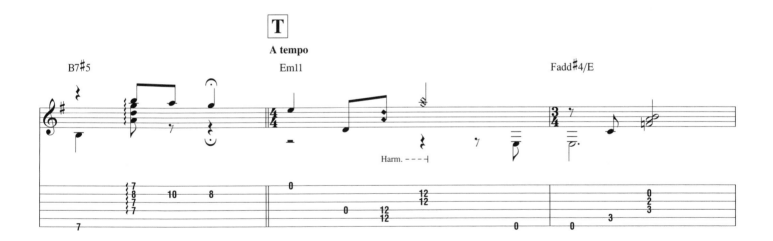

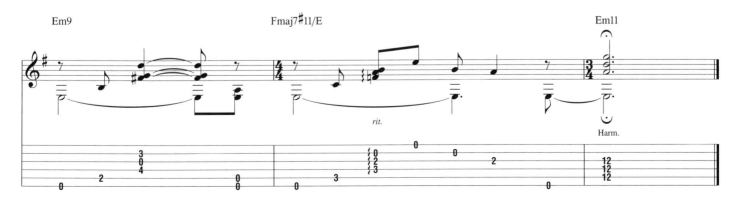

from Jimmy Raney - *But Beautiful*

Someone to Watch Over Me

Music and Lyrics by George Gershwin and Ira Gershwin

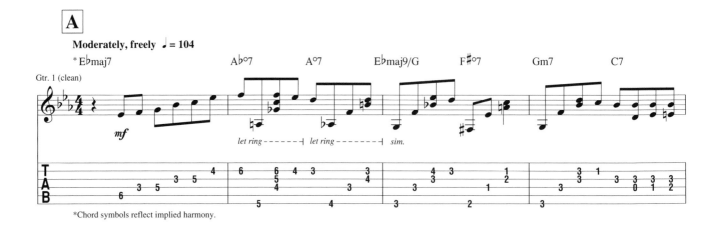

*Chord symbols reflect implied harmony.

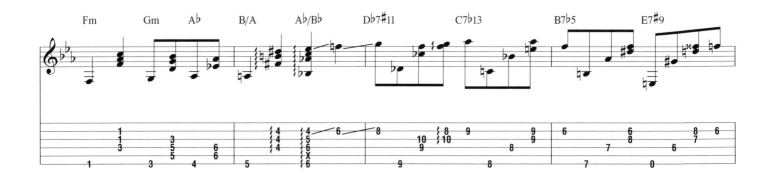

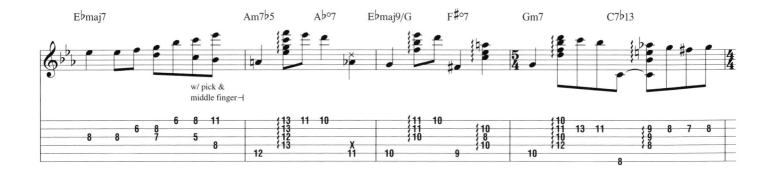

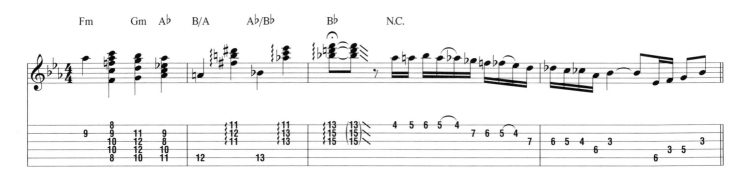

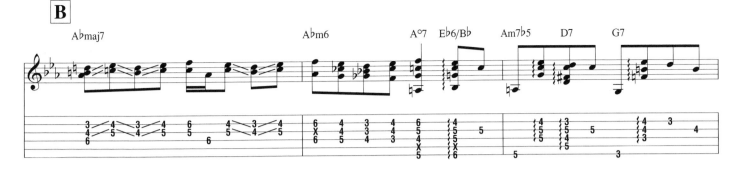

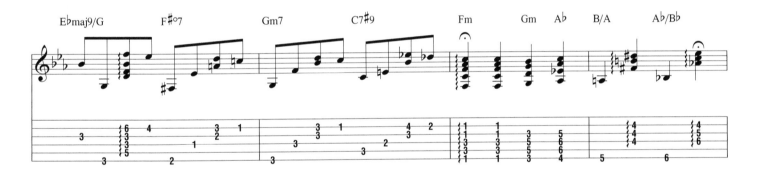

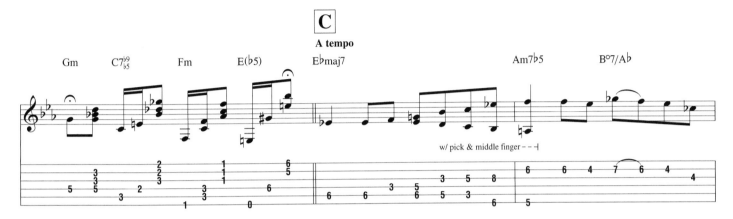

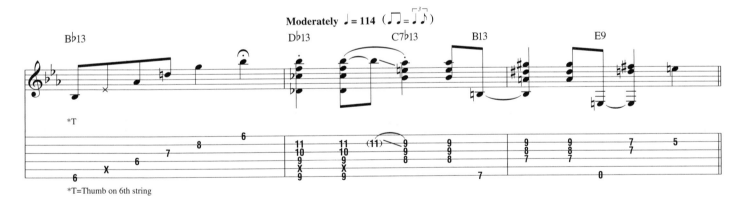

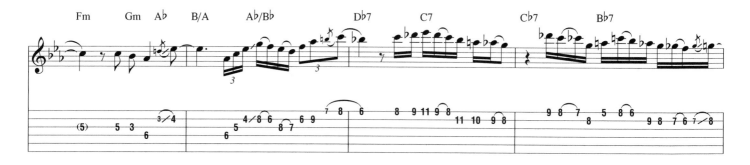

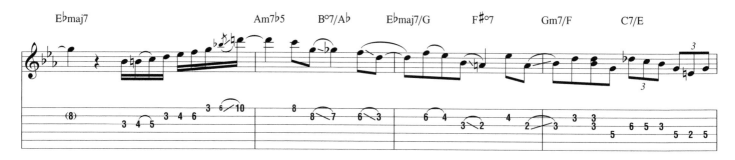

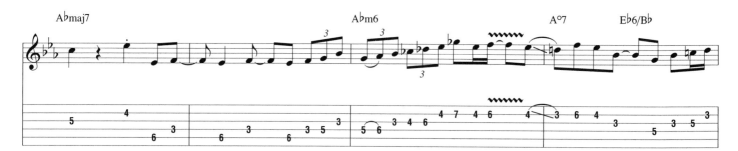

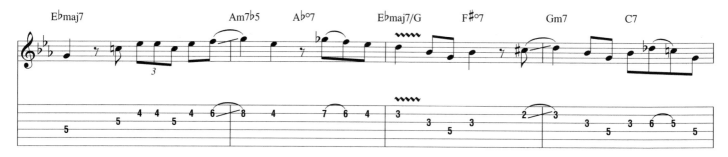

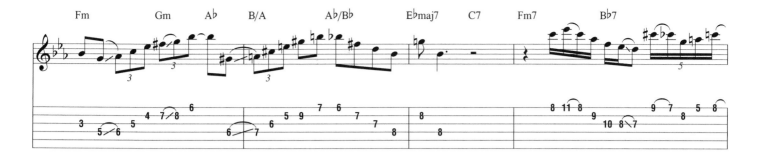

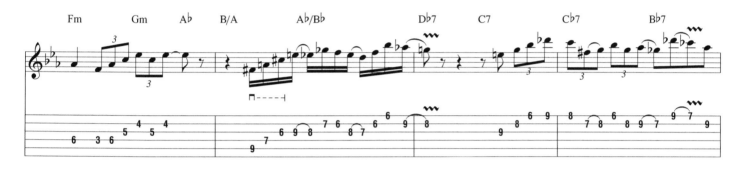

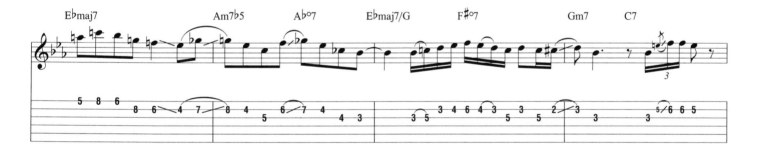

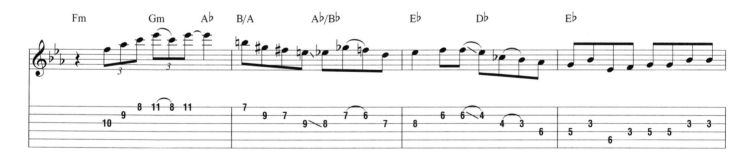

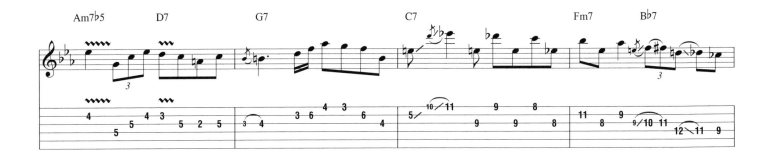

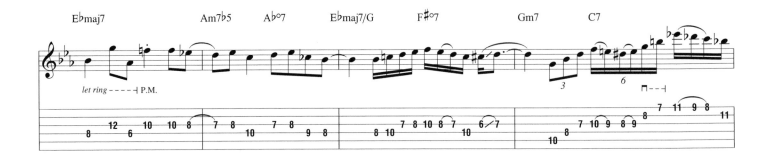

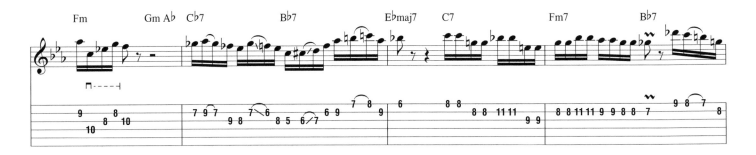

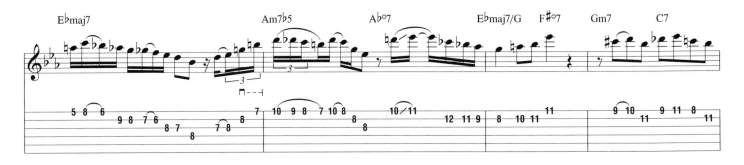

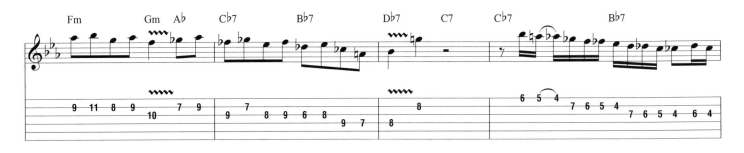

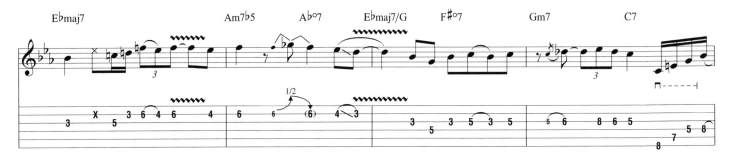

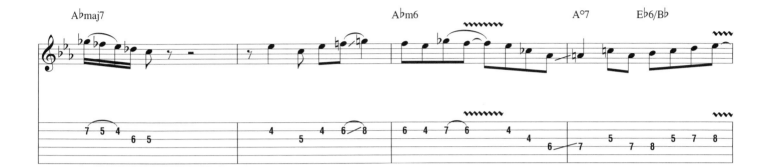

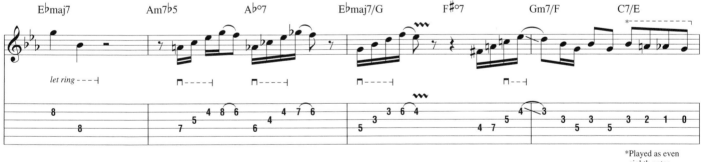

*Played as even
eighth notes.

E

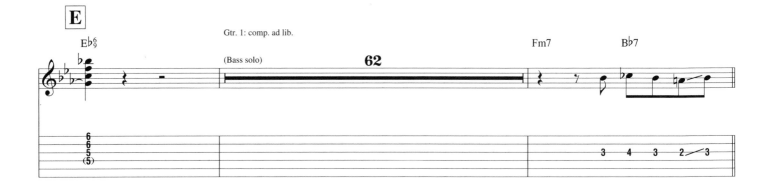

F

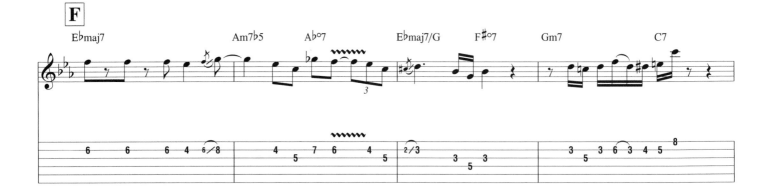

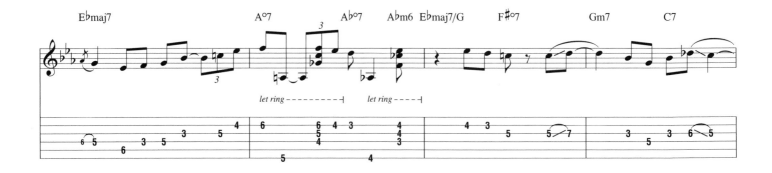

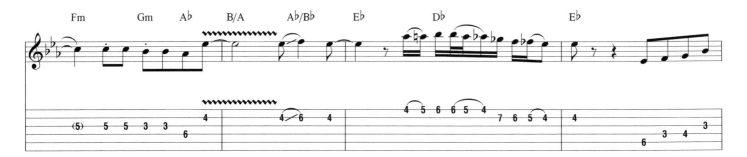

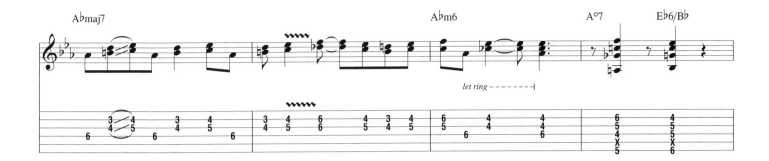

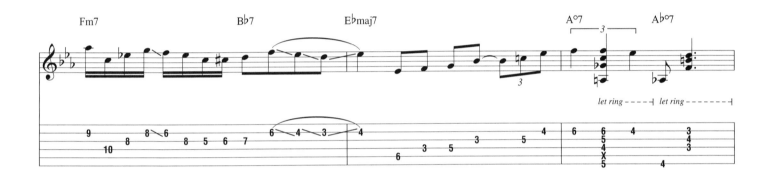

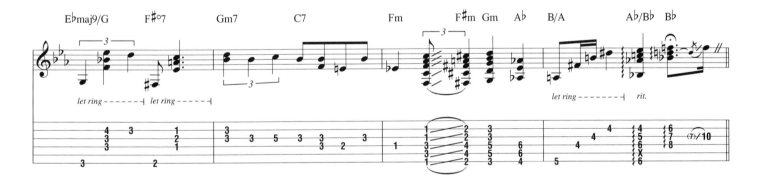

G

Slower ♩ = 84 (♫ = ♪♪)

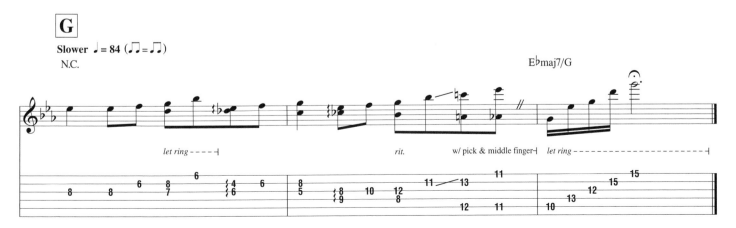

Summertime

from PORGY AND BESS

Music and Lyrics by George Gershwin, DuBose and Dorothy Heyward and Ira Gershwin

Tune down 1/4 step

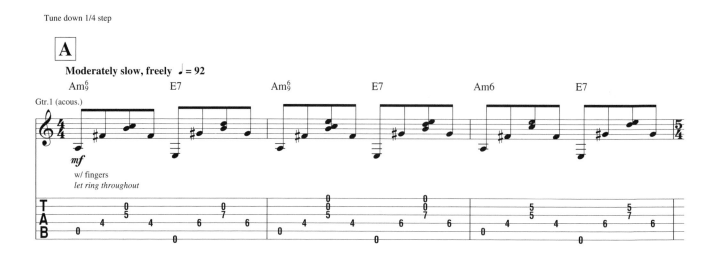

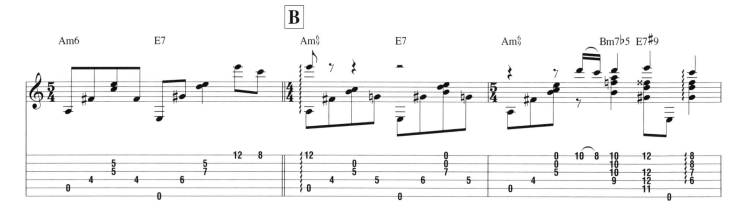

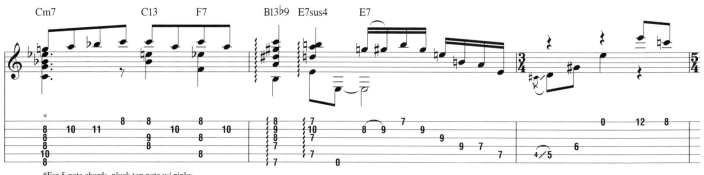

*For 5-note chords, pluck top note w/ pinky.

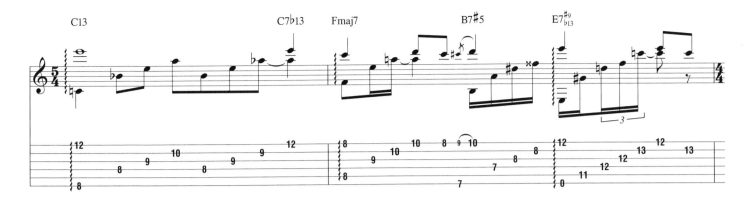

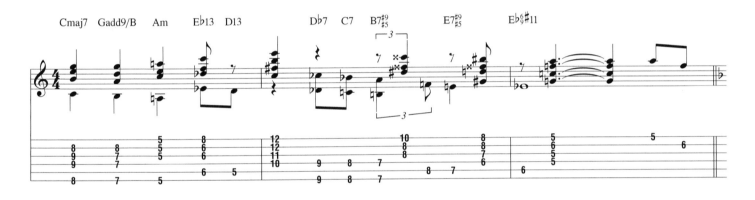

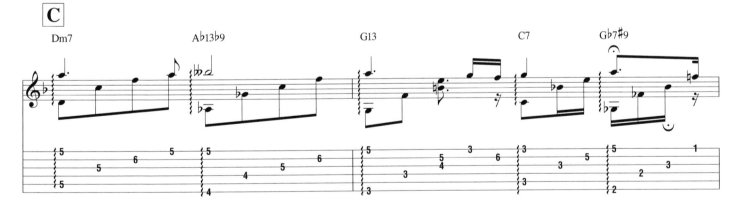

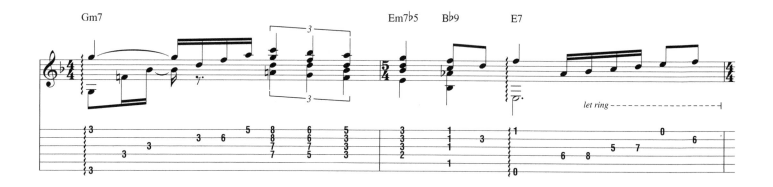

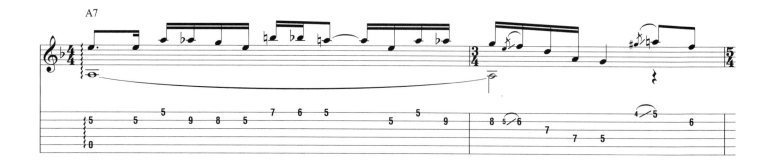

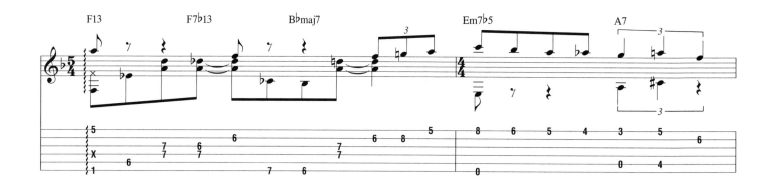

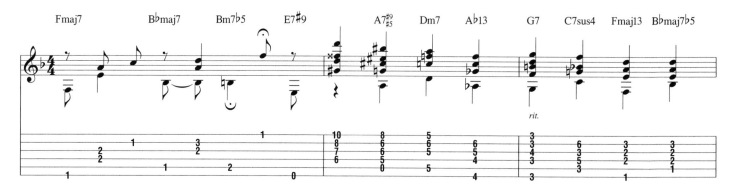

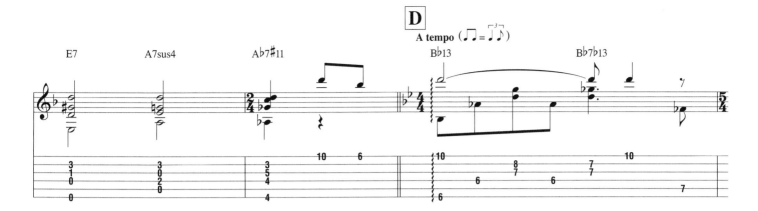

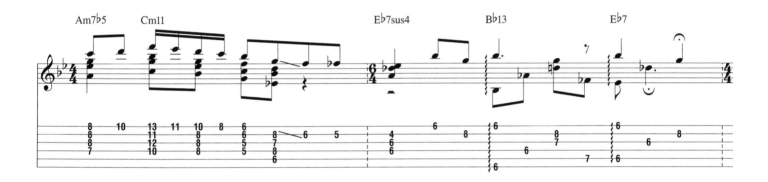

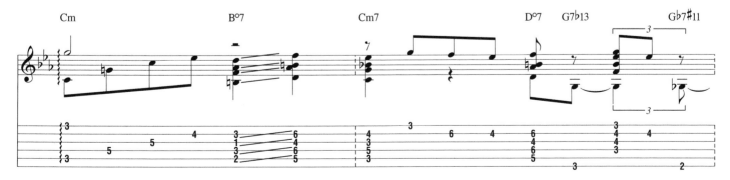

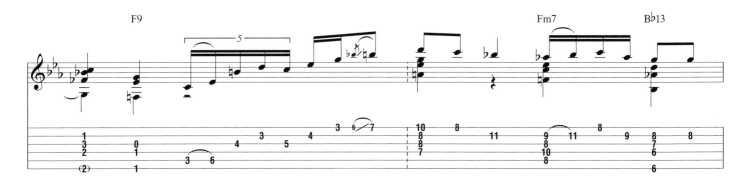

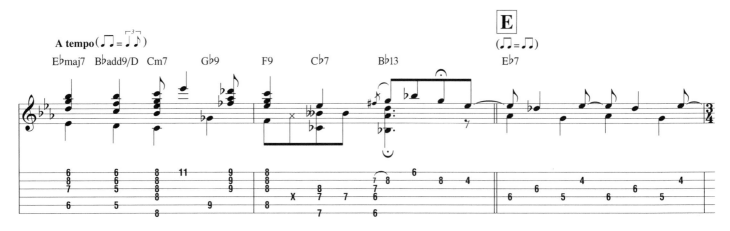

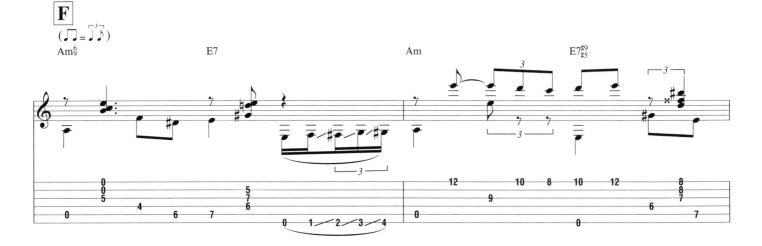

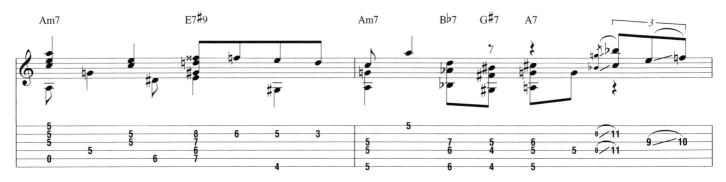

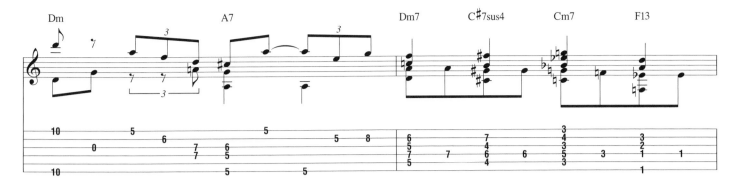

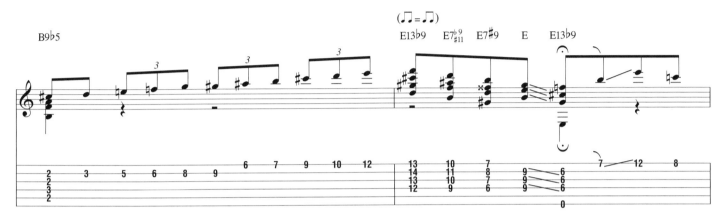

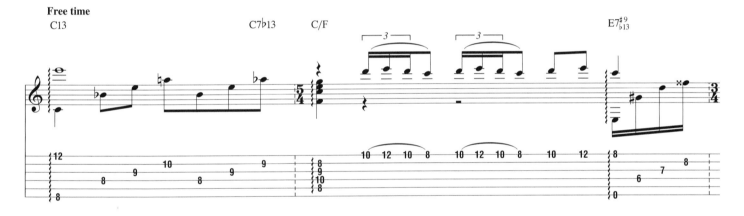

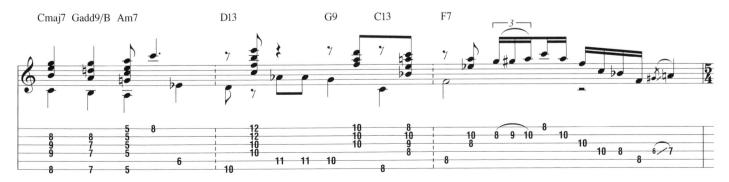

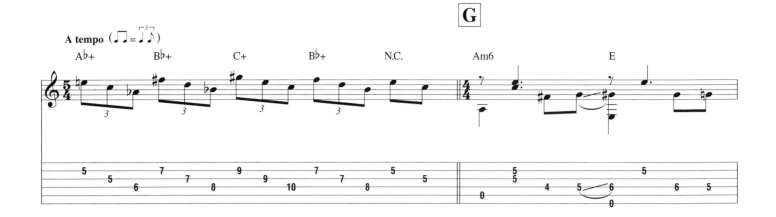

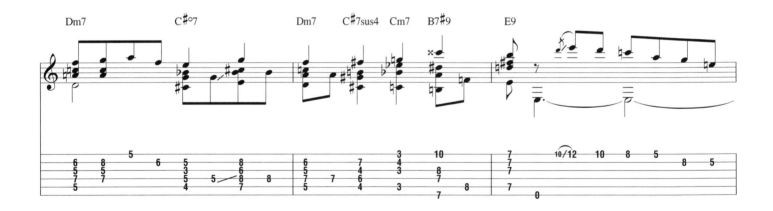

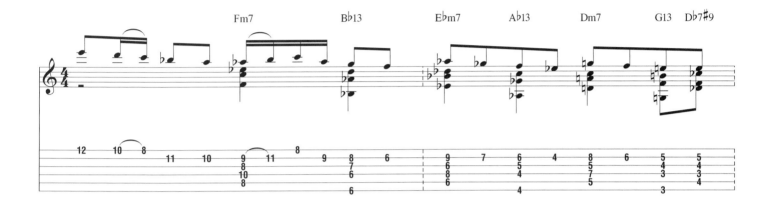

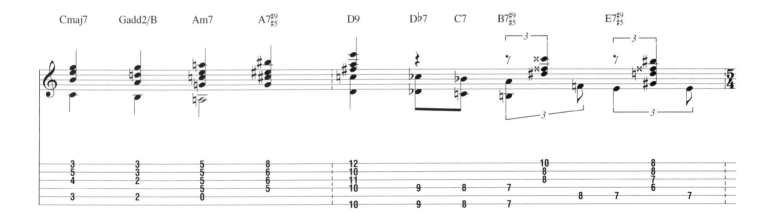

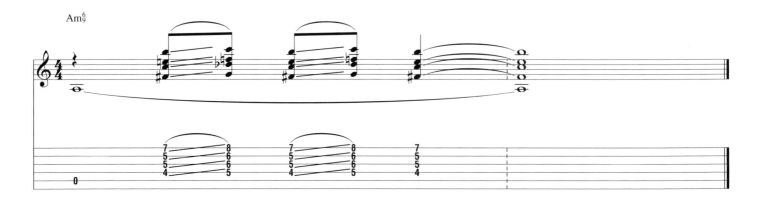

from Ted Greene - *Solo Guitar*

They Can't Take That Away from Me

Music and Lyrics by George Gershwin and Ira Gershwin

Tune down 1/2 step:
(low to high) E♭-A♭-D♭-G♭-B♭-E♭

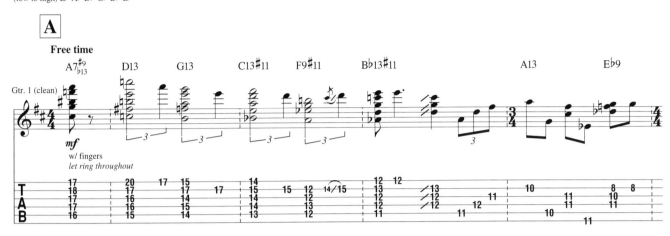

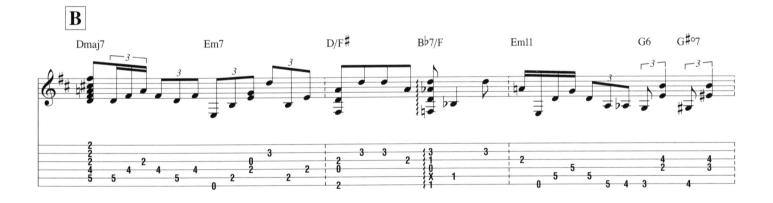

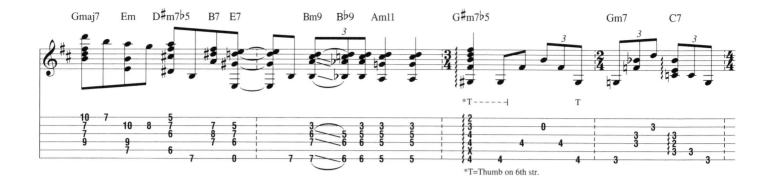

*T=Thumb on 6th str.

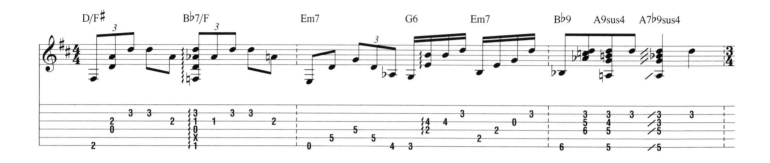

**Harp harmonics produced by lightly touching string
12 frets above fretted note while picking string.

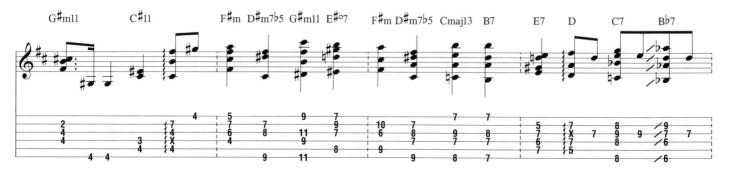

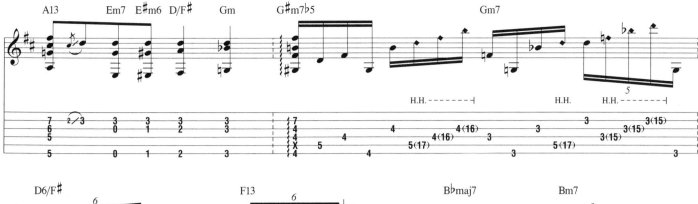

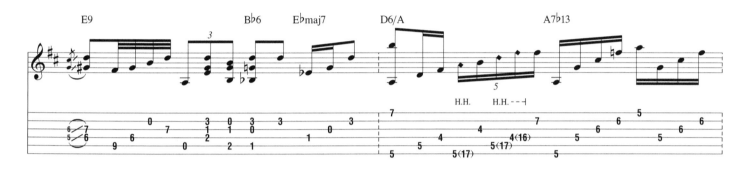

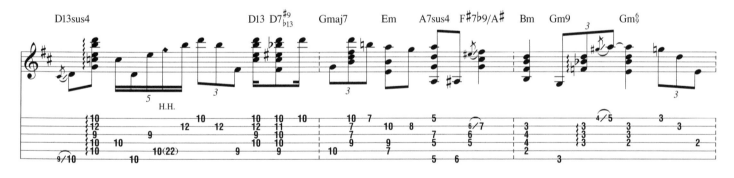

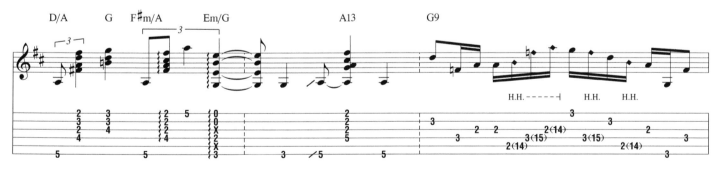

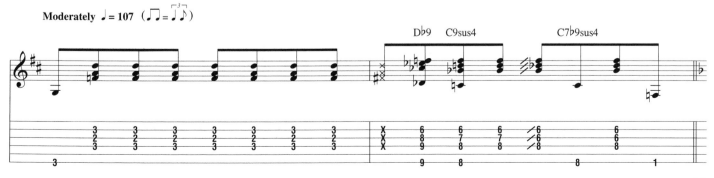

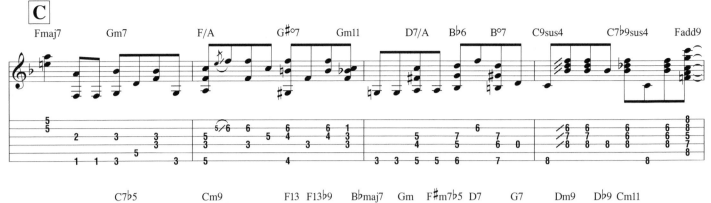

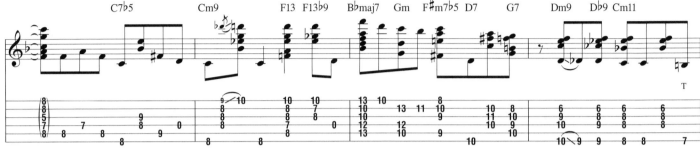

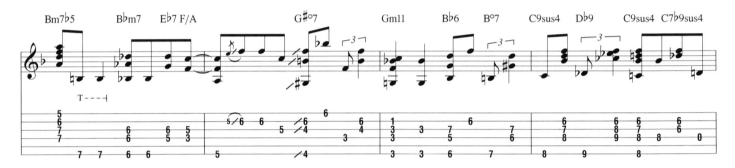

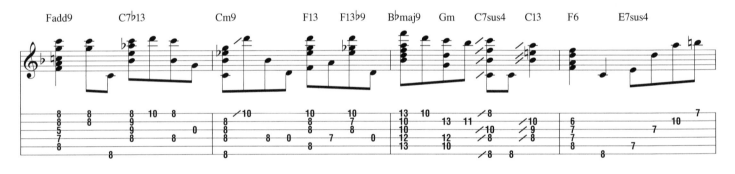

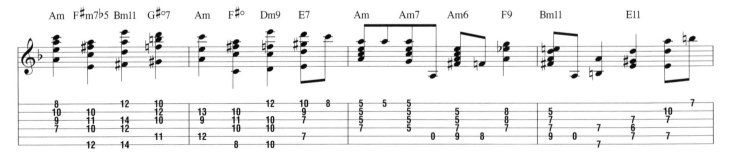

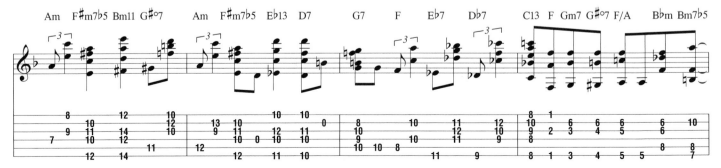

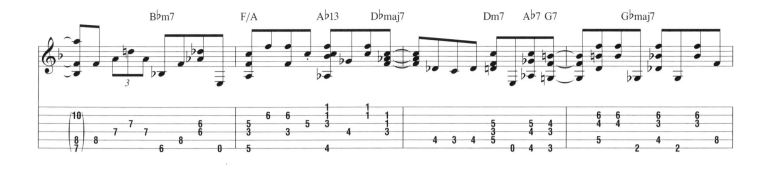

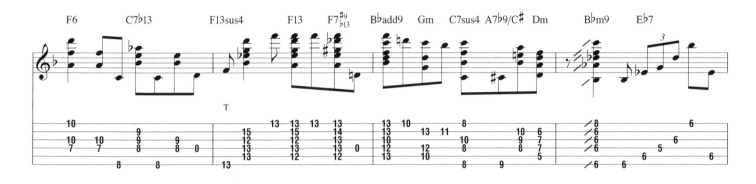

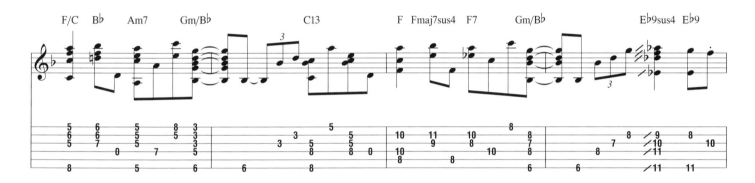

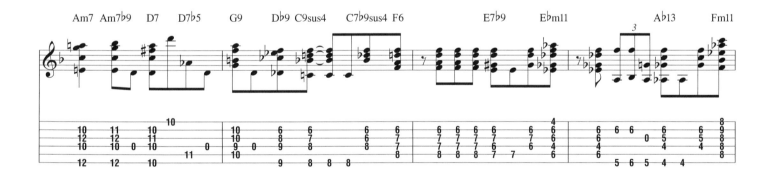

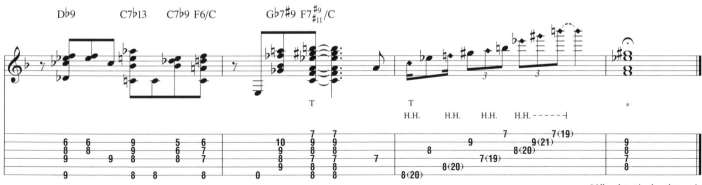

*Allow 1st-string harp harmonic
to "bleed" into and sustain
w/ chord, which is articulated
by slapping the pick-hand index
finger against the strings.

JAZZ GUITAR CHORD MELODY SOLOS

This series features chord melody arrangements in standard notation and tablature of songs for intermediate guitarists.

ALL-TIME STANDARDS **INCLUDES TAB**
27 songs, including: All of Me • Bewitched • Come Fly with Me • A Fine Romance • Georgia on My Mind • How High the Moon • I'll Never Smile Again • I've Got You Under My Skin • It's De-Lovely • It's Only a Paper Moon • My Romance • Satin Doll • The Surrey with the Fringe on Top • Yesterdays • and more.
00699757 Solo Guitar $14.99

CHRISTMAS CAROLS **INCLUDES TAB**
26 songs, including: Auld Lang Syne • Away in a Manger • Deck the Hall • God Rest Ye Merry, Gentlemen • Good King Wenceslas • Here We Come A-Wassailing • It Came upon the Midnight Clear • Joy to the World • O Holy Night • O Little Town of Bethlehem • Silent Night • Toyland • We Three Kings of Orient Are • and more.
00701697 Solo Guitar $12.99

DISNEY SONGS **INCLUDES TAB**
27 songs, including: Beauty and the Beast • Can You Feel the Love Tonight • Candle on the Water • Colors of the Wind • A Dream Is a Wish Your Heart Makes • Heigh-Ho • Some Day My Prince Will Come • Under the Sea • When You Wish upon a Star • A Whole New World (Aladdin's Theme) • Zip-A-Dee-Doo-Dah • and more.
00701902 Solo Guitar $14.99

DUKE ELLINGTON **INCLUDES TAB**
25 songs, including: C-Jam Blues • Caravan • Do Nothin' Till You Hear from Me • Don't Get Around Much Anymore • I Got It Bad and That Ain't Good • I'm Just a Lucky So and So • In a Sentimental Mood • It Don't Mean a Thing (If It Ain't Got That Swing) • Mood Indigo • Perdido • Prelude to a Kiss • Satin Doll • and more.
00700636 Solo Guitar $12.99

FAVORITE STANDARDS **INCLUDES TAB**
27 songs, including: All the Way • Autumn in New York • Blue Skies • Cheek to Cheek • Don't Get Around Much Anymore • How Deep Is the Ocean • I'll Be Seeing You • Isn't It Romantic? • It Could Happen to You • The Lady Is a Tramp • Moon River • Speak Low • Take the "A" Train • Willow Weep for Me • Witchcraft • and more.
00699756 Solo Guitar $14.99

FINGERPICKING JAZZ STANDARDS **INCLUDES TAB**
15 songs: Autumn in New York • Body and Soul • Can't Help Lovin' Dat Man • Easy Living • A Fine Romance • Have You Met Miss Jones? • I'm Beginning to See the Light • It Could Happen to You • My Romance • Stella by Starlight • Tangerine • The Very Thought of You • The Way You Look Tonight • When Sunny Gets Blue • Yesterdays.
00699840 Solo Guitar $7.99

JAZZ BALLADS **INCLUDES TAB**
27 songs, including: Body and Soul • Darn That Dream • Easy to Love (You'd Be So Easy to Love) • Here's That Rainy Day • In a Sentimental Mood • Misty • My Foolish Heart • My Funny Valentine • The Nearness of You • Stella by Starlight • Time After Time • The Way You Look Tonight • When Sunny Gets Blue • and more.
00699755 Solo Guitar $14.99

JAZZ CLASSICS **INCLUDES TAB**
27 songs, including: Blue in Green • Bluesette • Bouncing with Bud • Cast Your Fate to the Wind • Con Alma • Doxy • Epistrophy • Footprints • Giant Steps • Invitation • Lullaby of Birdland • Lush Life • A Night in Tunisia • Nuages • Ruby, My Dear • St. Thomas • Stolen Moments • Waltz for Debby • Yardbird Suite • and more.
00699758 Solo Guitar $14.99

Prices, content, and availability subject to change without notice. | Disney characters and artwork ©Disney Enterprises, Inc.

> *"Well-crafted arrangements that sound great and are still accessible to most players."*
> – *Guitar Edge* magazine

HAL•LEONARD®
www.halleonard.com